BRIDGING THE READING GAP

Acknowledgements

I am indebted to the hundreds of teachers I have worked with over the past 30 years. You have mentored me, encouraged me, and inspired me in so many ways. A special thank you to those who are currently in the field, tirelessly working toward shifting reading practices so that we can meet the needs of all learners. The complexities and the challenges that you face do not go unnoticed.

Thank you, Pembroke Publishers, for taking on another book written by me. You are traveling the shifting ground of reading instruction in Canada, and I love that you are committed to providing material that supports teachers in literacy work today.

To my editor, Joanne Close, thank you for the hours you have spent with this manuscript. You have been encouraging, provided insightful suggestions and are the deliverer of many fabulous text boxes! Your work has made this book more accessible for the teachers that will be using it. I love that you are a kindred literacy lover!

A special thanks to the teachers that tested lessons from this book at every stage or allowed me to teach these lessons in your classrooms. Your work and feedback have reshaped the presentation of material in its entirety. Dawn Ellingsen and Karen Samra, thank you for your early work with lessons and activities.

I am so thankful for the knowledge and insights shared by friend and colleague Dr. Kathryn Garforth, who generously read and provided feedback on Chapter 1. Meeting in person at IDA in Columbus, Ohio and the offer of top-shelf cider and your couch when my flight was laid over were just the beginnings of our adventures!

And finally, my family: Lorne, Ollie, Jana, Elissa, and Findley. Not only did you have to navigate the countless hours I spent at my laptop (in everyone's home) but also my ongoing distraction as I thought through how I could provide accessible material that supports teachers working with students in today's complex classrooms.

Bridging the Reading Gap

Explicit instruction that supports spelling, phonics, morphology, and vocabulary development in grades 4-8

Heather Willms

Pembroke Publishers Limited

This book is dedicated to Finley Willms.
I hope and trust that the work that 'teacher grandma' and fellow literacy leaders are doing today means that when you walk into your Kindergarten classroom in four short years, Structured Language and Literacy will be the only reading instruction you encounter.

© 2024 Pembroke Publishers
538 Hood Road
Markham, Ontario, Canada L3R 3K9
www.pembrokepublishers.com

All rights reserved.
No part of this publication may be reproduced in any form or by any means electronic or mechanical, including photocopy, scanning, recording, or any information, storage or retrieval system, without permission in writing from the publisher. Excerpts from this publication may be reproduced under licence from Access Copyright, or with the express written permission of Pembroke Publishers Limited, or as permitted by law.

Every effort has been made to contact copyright holders for permission to reproduce borrowed material. The publishers apologize for any such omissions and will be pleased to rectify them in subsequent reprints of the book.

Library and Archives Canada Cataloguing in Publication

Title: Bridging the reading gap : explicit instruction that supports spelling, phonics, morphology, and vocabulary development in grades 4–8 / Heather Willms.

Names: Willms, Heather, - author.

Description: Includes bibliographical references and index.

Identifiers: Canadiana (print) 20240342240 | Canadiana (ebook) 20240342313 | ISBN 9781551383675 (softcover) | ISBN 9781551389677 (PDF)

Subjects: LCSH: Reading (Elementary)

Classification: LCC LB1573 .W55 2024 | DDC 372.41—dc23

Editor: Joanne Close
Cover Design: John Zehethofer
Typesetting: Jay Tee Graphics Ltd.

Printed and bound in Canada
9 8 7 6 5 4 3 2 1

Contents

Introduction 7

Chapter 1: Teaching Reading 8
Today's Classrooms 8
How Students Learn to Read – The Science of Reading 11
A Look at the Big 5 13
Structured Language and Literacy 15
Screening and Assessments: The Why, What, and When of Screening 16
Structure of this Resource 24
Summary 26

Chapter 2: Vocabulary 27
The Learning Progression of Vocabulary 27
The Three Tiers of Vocabulary 29
Teaching Tier 2 Vocabulary 30
Word Storage for Retrieval 30
Learning Words in Context 31
Functional Vocabulary 31
Synonyms, Antonyms, Homonyms, Homophones, Homographs… and Heteronyms 32
Morphology 32
Idioms 33
Oxymorons 33
Activities to Build Vocabulary Knowledge and Skills 34
Lessons 43
Worksheets 47

Chapter 3: Morphology 56
Why Morphology? 56
Affixes 57
Greek Combining Forms 61
Shifting Syllable Stress 63
Connecting Vowel Letters 63
Seven Practices 64
Lessons 66
Next Steps in Morphology 75
Activities 75

Worksheets *81*

Chapter 4: Spelling *93*

A Teacher's Love/Hate Relationship with Spelling *93*
Encoding and Decoding *94*
Why Spelling? *95*
Where Do I Start? *97*
Lesson Word Lists *98*
Multiple Ways to Mark Spelling *100*
Spelling Lesson Format *101*
Activities *101*
Lessons *110*
Worksheets *143*

Chapter 5: Multisyllable Words *147*

The 6 Syllable Rules *147*
Foundational Knowledge for Working with Multisyllable Words *148*
The Animal Strategies *149*
Teaching Syllabication *150*
Lessons *151*
Worksheets *163*

Recommended Resources *167*

References *172*

Index *176*

Introduction

The concept for this book began five years ago when I made a comment while presenting at a professional development workshop. I was working with teachers from Grades K–8 when an upper elementary teacher asked how they could explicitly teach reading when they have such a broad range of reading skills in their classes. What could they do to help all students become better readers without taking significant amounts of time from their Language Arts block? This question resonated with me, a former Grade 5 teacher, as explicit literacy instruction is the number one thing I would change if I were to teach Grade 5 again. I responded that I would address explicit vocabulary, morphology, and spelling instruction through my spelling program. We, as upper elementary teachers, understand spelling and it is often a part of our weekly schedule.

The workshop moved on, but when I opened my email the next day my inbox had blown up with upper elementary/middle school teachers asking which spelling program I would recommend. I was the district Reading Intervention Teacher for Comox Valley Schools at the time, and my primary task was to support classroom and Learning Support teachers with reading instruction. I took the question seriously and began a two-year quest to find a spelling program where teachers could teach spelling and address word meaning and construction at the same time. I wanted something that did not require a significant amount of preparation, aligned with reading research, and could be embedded into the routines of an upper elementary/middle school classroom.

That was 2020 and the only programs I felt ticked the boxes of explicit instruction (and there were several good ones) were programs where students needed individual workbooks. In a world of limited funding for resources, I knew these programs would be cost prohibitive. I continued to work in upper elementary and middle school classrooms, teaching and modeling explicit vocabulary, morphology, and phonics instruction, and writing lessons for the classes I worked in.

That work has led to the material that you will find in *Bridging the Reading Gap*. It is a collection of instructional practices I would use if I were teaching an upper elementary/middle school class today. It is a starting place for upper elementary/middle school teachers working with today's students.

1

Teaching Reading

When starting to write this manuscript, I initially built lessons that combined vocabulary, morphology, decoding, and spelling. They were long and complex lessons and they put significant demands on the teacher delivering the lessons. In this book's evolved state, these important components of reading have been pulled apart and placed in separate chapters and lessons. I encourage you to start where you feel comfortable and continue to build skills as you explore chapters throughout the book.

An attempt has been made to keep concepts simple and manageable for complex classrooms where there is a range of reading abilities. Word lists contain everyday language and complex language used across curriculums. There are entry points for students with a breadth of skill levels like emergent lists and scaffolded worksheets.

By starting to teach reading explicitly at the classroom level, you will provide strategies and knowledge that students can rely on when they encounter challenging words and/or text. You will see it begin to close the skill gap in reading abilities in your classroom.

Today's Classrooms

Teaching reading in today's classroom can be challenging—and rewarding—for a number of reasons. To begin, there are significant differences between reading instruction for Grades K–3 and Grades 4–8. For many of you reading this book, you will be teaching in those latter grades and may find yourself facing the following factors when preparing and delivering lessons for your students:

The Skill Spread

Since students have been in school longer, there is a greater range of skills within a classroom. When I taught Grade 5, I had students who were sounding out simple CVC words (Consonant-Vowel-Consonant words like *fin* and *man*), I had students who were reading at a high school level, and I had everything in between. That remains true today.

Declining Reading Abilities

When I started teaching Grade 5 in 2001, almost all my students could read at, or close to, grade level. During those early years, it was common for my students to engage in small-group novel reading or to read an article or book independently. In the years I had a nonreading student, they would go to the Learning Support teacher for instruction while I worked with the rest of the class.

By the time I left the classroom in 2018, approximately 45 percent of my students were reading below grade level, with 4 to 6 students having emergent reading skills. As a Learning Support teacher in the years following, I was overwhelmed with lists of students who needed reading intervention.

There have been multiple studies confirming this decline. While the COVID pandemic (masks, missing school, online instruction) did not initiate concerns over dropping reading scores, it did expedite the decline. PISA (OECD Programme for International Student Assessment) conducts rigorous international surveys of student knowledge and skills in 81 countries. PISA 2022 scores show a drop in every Canadian province between 2018 and 2022.

Comparisons of performance in PISA 2018 and 2022: READING				
Canada, province, or OECD average	2018		2022	
	Average	Standard error	Average	Standard error
Canada	**520**	**(1.8)**	**507***	**(2.5)**
Newfoundland and Labrador	512	(4.3)	478*	(7.2)
Prince Edward Island	503	(8.3)	496	(10.4)
Nova Scotia	516	(3.9)	489*	(6.4)
New Brunswick	489	(3.5)	469*	(4.3)
Quebec	519	(3.5)	501*	(4.9)
Ontario	524	(3.5)	512*	(4.1)
Manitoba	494	(3.4)	486	(4.1)
Saskatchewan	499	(3.0)	484*	(4.3)
Alberta	532	(4.3)	525	(6.4)
British Columbia	519	(4.5)	511	(6.0)
OECD average	**487**	**(0.4)**	**477***	**(1.5)**

* Statistically significant differences compared with PISA 2018.
Note: The linkage error is incorporated into the standard error for 2022. The composition of OECD countries varies from cycle to cycle; therefore, in trend analyses, the OECD average is adjusted to reflect changes in that composition.

Source: *Council of Ministers of Education. (2023.)* Measuring Up: Canadian results of the OECD PISA 2022 study, *p. 233.*

There is also much data showing that these gaps are not only academic, but developmental as well (Mayo Clinic, 2023).

If we add technology (gaming and social media), absenteeism, anxiety, childhood depression, food and housing insecurity, and complex family dynamics to the mix, it is little wonder that teachers are struggling to meet the diverse needs of their students.

Teaching Reading and/or Teaching Content

The decline in reading abilities greatly impacted how I taught over my 17 years in Grade 5. Each year, I adjusted my content and instructional strategies to meet the needs of my students. By 2018, I was reading everything aloud because I understood my role to be teaching content. If I read instructions and texts to the class, they would all have access to the content I was working with. I thought teaching reading was the job of early elementary teachers. I was a Grade 5 teacher after all and not only did I believe it was not my job to teach reading, but I also had no idea how to do it!

Knowledge and Strategies Around Teaching Reading

Like myself, many upper elementary/middle school teachers do not have the training and skill set to teach reading. This has nothing to do with competency and/or a desire to learn. Upper elementary/middle school teachers either have not been trained to teach reading or have not sought professional development in how to teach reading because they did not plan to teach early elementary (or both).

There is also a misconception that reading and spelling acquisition happens with exposure to text and there is a lack of understanding around explicit instruction and its role in supporting reading growth. In my work as a university instructor, I want all students in my literacy classes to know the why and how of teaching reading because there is important reading instruction that happens beyond the early grades—vocabulary, morphology, and etymology, to name a few.

For upper elementary/middle school teachers, it would be helpful to start looking at reading instruction like any other content area—it needs to be taught. Due to significant reading lags in almost every classroom today, **we are all teaching reading.**

What is exciting about teaching reading at this age level is that through explicit instruction many students will quickly learn the patterns and intricacies of the English language. Barring a reading disability, students will see growth quite quickly and become excited about language and literacy.

Age Level Material for Teaching Reading

While there are copious amounts of excellent material for teaching reading to early elementary students, there is a corresponding dearth of material for upper elementary/middle school. Older students do not want to work with material that has 'cutesy' pictures of cartoon children, bunnies, and puppies, but they may still need the content that these materials contain. Finding appropriate material that meets the needs of older readers, or creating it, is a challenge and takes time.

The Confidence to Grow as Readers

I have worked with hundreds of early readers, and I have yet to meet a child who did not want to learn to read. I cannot say this of my work with upper elementary/middle school students who may experience a lack of desire to read because they feel that they cannot learn.

As an interventionist, I have met many students in Grades 4 and above who have given up on learning to read. They have worked hard to figure it out for several years, many receiving small-group instruction, but they know they are not good at it. They have lost confidence, find activities difficult, and find it socially challenging to either hide or minimize their inability to read well. They are embarrassed to be pulled into small groups because they have done it for years and they know it has not helped them. Add to this material that they describe as "babyish," and we find ourselves having to build courage and stamina in struggling readers before getting to the actual teaching of reading.

Complex Classrooms

And finally, it is important that we acknowledge the shift toward more complex behaviours and needs in today's classrooms. I often share that if you were to have walked into a Grade 5 classroom 15 years ago, students were likely engaged and on task. If you were to walk into a Grade 5 classroom today and students are engaged and on task, what it took for the educator to achieve and maintain that classroom dynamic is different. It now takes more vigilance, energy, relationship-building with students/parents, and social emotional knowledge/strategies/skills than it did 15 years ago just to maintain a calm, engaging classroom. Complex children mean more meetings, more paperwork, and more preparation than a mere 15 years ago. This has a significant impact on preparation and the ability to simply deliver instruction.

How Students Learn to Read – The Science of Reading

> "Informed teachers are our best insurance against reading failure. While programs are very helpful tools, programs don't teach, teachers do."
> Linguist and educator Louisa Moats (2020)

Understanding how students learn to read empowers you, the educator, to make the decisions necessary to support your students. Your knowledge will guide your instruction toward evidence-based practices and resources, and away from those that are inaccurate and less effective in reading instruction.

Reading is a human invention. Unlike speech, which the typically developing brain comes equipped for, there is no part of the brain that is specifically designed for reading. This means reading requires use of brain areas designed for other functions. When children learn to read, new neuro pathways are built. One of the awe-inspiring things about teaching reading is that we are essentially rewiring brains!

The Simple View of Reading and Scarborough's Rope

Decoding x Language Comprehension = Reading Comprehension

The Simple View of Reading (SVR) (Gough & Tunmer, 1986) and Scarborough's Reading Rope (Scarborough, 2001) are excellent places to start when it comes to understanding what is needed when students learn to read. SVR indicates that for students to read and understand, they must have the skills to decode a passage and the language to understand it. Without one or the other, it is not possible to read with understanding, which is the goal of reading!

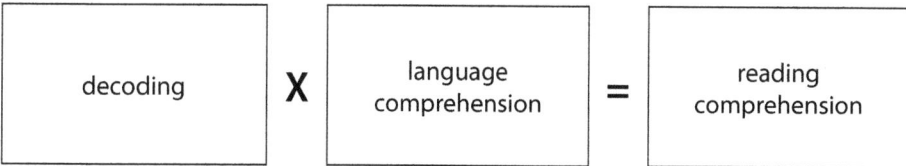

This model is further expanded by Hollis Scarborough's Reading Rope, which shows the micro skills that make up decoding and language comprehension in the SVR.

The following graphic, created by Dr. Kim St. Martin and her team at Michigan's MTSS Technical Assistance Center, shows the reading rope and its alignment with grade-level instruction. Although components of reading are introduced in the early grades, we continue to strengthen and hone these skills in upper elementary/middle school classrooms. It is only when early reading skills are solidified that educators can fully focus on higher order cognitive skills. If foundational work has not been done, it impedes comprehension of complex texts encountered in later grades. As these micro skills are strengthened, so is reading and comprehension.

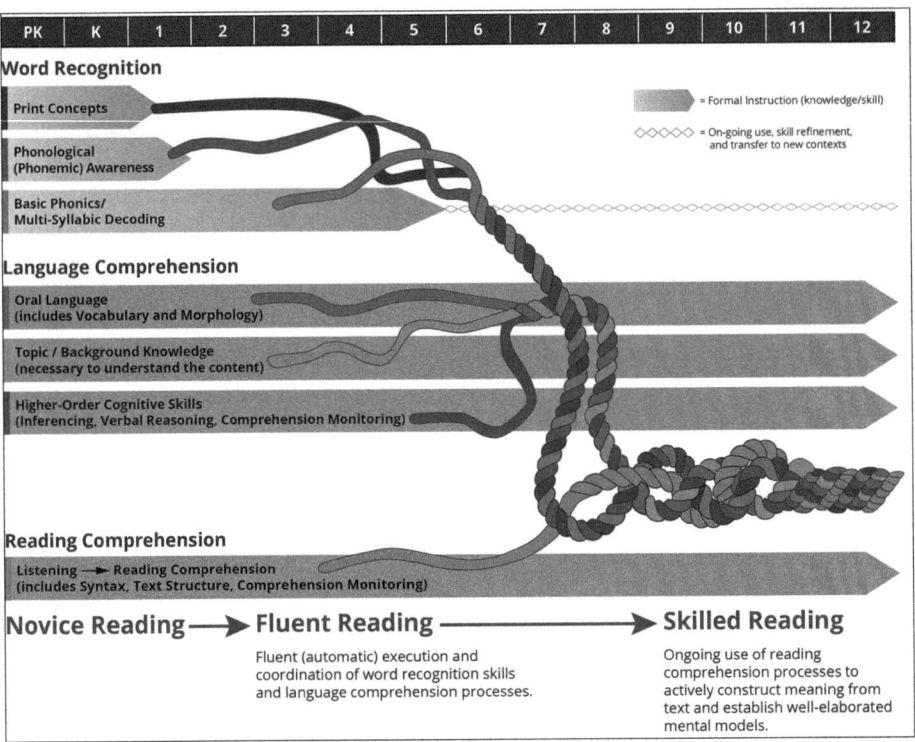

Used with permission of Dr. Kimberly St. Martin

As this graphic illustrates, decoding and language comprehension are not the only things that contribute to reading success, and as a Grade 5 teacher (and someone who knew little about how a child learns to read), I would have found a model such as this helpful. Checking to see if students have a decoding or language concern would have begun to guide my instruction and directed where and how I supported my students. It would also have helped me group my students according to need and skill gaps rather than reading level.

Orthographic Mapping

Ortho = straight Graphy = written

It is important to take a brief look at Orthographic Mapping (OM) before we move on, because it plays a significant role in word storage and retrieval for reading and spelling. If this is your first introduction to OM, you may want to look at additional reliable sources that provide further detail. (See the resource list on page 170.)

OM is the process of forming sound-to-letter connections to combine and recall the spelling, pronunciation, and meaning of words (Kilpatrick, 2016). It is a process where children learn to read words at a glance, spell from memory, and develop and store vocabulary. As children store words for instant retrieval, they build a bank of words they can instantly draw from called an orthographic lexicon. The more they know about a word (e.g., spelling, meaning, source) the deeper and richer the lexicon.

Respected reading researcher Linnea Ehri states that orthographic mapping is when "connections are formed that link the spelling of written words to their pronunciations and meaning in memory" (2013). In other words, strings of letters are attached to sounds, which form words, which in turn have meaning.

Once students begin to map and store words (OM), it allows them to read words in a fraction of a second and with this process in place, they can map and store new words through one to four exposures in text.

All of this is to say that explicit, evidence-based reading instruction contributes to the storing of words in the brain. This is quite different than previously held theories that proposed reading as a visual process. In fact, words are not stored visually but are stored in the much larger oral filing system of the brain (Kilpatrick, 2016).

Many reading support teachers work with older students (Grades 4 and up) who are still decoding every word on the page. A sign that orthographic mapping is not in place is when a student decodes a word in text, and then needs to decode the same word on the next page, and then again on the next. While typically developing readers may need one to four exposures to a word to map and store it, struggling readers may need 12, 30, 50, or even hundreds of exposures to store words for automatic retrieval. This does not mean the work cannot be done, it just takes more time and more exposure to a word.

A Look at the Big 5

After the Simple View of Reading and Scarborough's Reading Rope, it is important to know and understand the Big 5 of reading instruction. So, what are they and how did they come to be so important?

Due to dropping reading scores in the US, the country's Congress mandated a panel comprising scientists in reading research, teachers, college representatives, administrators, and parents to assess the effectiveness of different approaches to teaching reading and make recommendations. The panel looked at over 100,000 research studies and published results (NIH, 2000). While this report received a significant amount of press, other nations have done similar reviews and come to the same conclusion (e.g., the Rose Report in the UK, Right to Read in Ontario, and the National Inquiry into the Teaching of Literacy in Australia).

Its findings highlight five key components or pillars of effective and comprehensive reading instruction:

- Phonemic Awareness
- Phonics
- Fluency
- Vocabulary
- Comprehension

While we pull these components apart to analyze them, it is important to understand that they not only work together, but there is a dynamic interplay between them.

A sixth component—active, self-regulatory processes—has been proposed by Duke and Cartwright (2021). While this pillar does not have years of research and practice behind it, it resonates with the work of upper elementary/middle school teachers.

Phonemic Awareness

> **Phonemic Awareness**: the ability to recognize and manipulate the smallest units of a spoken word (the phoneme).
>
> **Phonological Awareness**: An umbrella term that addresses the ability to recognize and manipulate the spoken parts of sentences and words. It includes rhyming, alliteration, dividing syllables, and phonemes (individual sounds).

There are two terms that are often used when talking about sounds in words: **Phonemic Awareness** and **Phonological Awareness**. Sometimes they will be used interchangeably, but they are not the same thing.

The English language is made up of approximately 44 phonemes (depending on dialect), and it is important that students can identify and manipulate phonemes in order to match these sounds with letters on the page.

Explicit practice with phonemic awareness in the early grades builds a strong knowledge base for reading (decoding) and an understanding of how words are put together for spelling (encoding). Strong phonemic awareness skills enable readers to isolate, blend, segment, and flex sounds when they come across new words and seek to match them with the words they have heard and/or spoken.

Most upper elementary/middle school students will have some level of phonemic awareness and those that struggle with this skill are probably already working with some type of reading support but... not always!!!

One place you will see phonemic awareness concerns is with missing letters in spelling. Can students hear all the sounds and therefore represent them on the page? You will find oral activities in several spelling lessons that highlight awareness of the sounds in target words.

Phonics

A simple way to describe phonics is that words are made up of sounds (phonemic awareness) and letters represent those sounds. When addressing phonics, students begin by learning the sounds of the 26 letters of the alphabet and their names. Since there are approximately 44 phonemes, and only 26 letters, we deal with the extra phonemes by combining letters to represent sounds. This is an oversimplification, but it makes sense to students and helps them to understand the code of our English language. This gets even more complicated when we learn that multiple letter combinations can represent one sound (*late, bay, sleigh*, and *main* all have the long /a/ sound) and one letter combination can represent multiple sounds (*bough, dough, slough, thought*). There are approximately 230 letter combinations (graphemes) to spell the sounds in speech (Mather et al., 2009)!

When students learn to read by matching sounds to letters and begin to decode, we often say they have "broken the code." They have made the connection that the marks on the page (which represent sounds) can be combined to match the words that they speak (the alphabetic principle), and that's what reading is all about. A Grade 1 colleague once shared with me that a student exclaimed, "The letters are talking," when they realized that the letters matched the words they spoke. They clearly understood the connection between speech and text.

While some students may learn to read with broad literacy instruction, a significant contributor to a deep understanding of how the English language is put together comes from explicit instruction in phonics (which benefits all learners). Reading and writing are linguistic work, as students are learning the English language system that they use every day in speech.

Fluency

Fluency is the ability to read quickly (at the rate of speaking), accurately and with expression. When students read with expression, it indicates that they understand what they are reading. Strong fluency skills are an indicator that all is well in the decoding and comprehension world, as it draws on a combination of skills.

Students who read fluently can see through the text to the story behind it. Students who are not fluent use so much mental desk space to decode that they are not able to see through to the story beyond the text.

The bank of stored words that a student brings to the text (their orthographic lexicon) impacts their fluency skills. The goal is to have a large bank of stored words so that they recognize them accurately and automatically in print. This is not done by memorizing words by sight but through orthographic mapping.

Vocabulary

Vocabulary is the recognition and understanding of the meaning of words. Students who recognize, understand, and can use many words are considered to have a large or broad vocabulary (orthographic lexicon), whereas students who have a small or limited vocabulary recognize, understand, and use a small bank of words. Vocabulary is explored more deeply in Chapter 2.

Comprehension

Comprehension, or understanding what a text is communicating, is the goal of reading and is the reason we read. While there are several important pieces that contribute to comprehension (for example, background knowledge and knowledge of the text structure), the other Big 4 are also building blocks of comprehension. It is not uncommon for teachers to choose to teach comprehension skills (e.g., main idea, inferring, sequencing) that have been found to have minimal impact on reading comprehension (Shanahan, 2018), without realizing that a lack of fluency, decoding skills, and vocabulary may be the factors that are impeding a student's comprehension. You will notice that the Big 5 are enfolded into the vocabulary, morphology, and spelling lessons and activities found within this book. This is intentional as rich connections between the Big 5 contribute to powerful, effective instruction and growing strong readers.

Structured Language and Literacy

Besides the term Science of Reading, you have probably heard the term Structured Literacy or Structured Language and Literacy. Structured Language and Literacy is built on the knowledge gained through reading research. It is reading instruction that is systematic, explicit, engaging, and success oriented. This is not the same as a Balanced Literacy approach, which focuses on guiding, sharing, and independent reading.

> ### Hallmarks of Structured Language and Literacy
>
> - While children learn to speak naturally, reading and writing must be taught. With explicit instruction, the teacher provides clear and precise instruction and modeling of each concept.
> - Systematic means that the teacher follows a scope and sequence or learning progression for introducing each skill. There is ongoing review of skills previously taught and mastered. The sequence of skills moves from simple, prerequisite concepts to advanced skills. This is a shift from broad instruction at the classroom level and explicit instruction in intervention.
> - The teacher spends a significant amount of time on instruction and coaching, with a minimal amount of time where students are learning on their own. Materials and resources support explicit, systematic instruction.
> - Ongoing progress monitoring and assessment informs the teacher of skills gained and those that need additional instruction and practice. It informs the teacher on what they need to adjust in their instructional practices to meet the needs of their students.
> - Success-oriented instruction sees the teacher providing corrective feedback when errors occur.
> - It is student data-driven instruction and practice, where collected data provides information regarding student skills that require further instruction and growth.
>
> *Concepts Addressed in Structured Language and Literacy*
>
> - Phonology: Study of sounds in spoken words
> - Sound-to-symbol relationship: Relationship between speech sounds and letters
> - Syllables: Understanding there are different ways to divide words into syllables
> - Syntax: Grammatical order of words
> - Word Study
>   - Semantics: Understanding the meaning of words and sentences
>   - Morphology: Study of word parts
>   - Orthography: How words are spelled
>   - Etymology: Word origins

Screening and Assessments: The Why, What, and When of Screening

Reading screening can be tricky. A key component of reading screening/assessment often means the teacher is sitting one-on-one with a student listening to them read. This can seem almost impossible in complex and busy classrooms. As challenging as this is, how will teachers know where their students are in their reading journey if they do not listen to them read?

Screening starts with asking, "What do I want to know?" In the early grades, it is important to determine who is at risk of struggling with reading and which students are lagging in skills. In upper elementary/middle school, educators want to know if they have students who are lagging and if yes how far they might be reading below grade level. Are they just slightly behind or are they well below expectations for their grade? Once educators determine who is below grade level, their number one question is, "What can I do to bridge the gap?" That is where assessment enters the picture.

Multi-Tiered System of Supports (MTSS) Reading Assessments

Many schools are working with MTSS (Multi-Tiered System of Supports), which is a strength-based, proactive, and preventative framework that merges data and instruction to support students (mtss4success.org). If your school is not using MTSS, it is well worth exploring. Within this system, there are four types of reading assessments:

- universal screeners
- diagnostic assessments
- progress monitoring tools
- summative assessments

A **universal screener** is administered 1 to 3 times a year for every student in the class. The intention is to identify readers who are at risk and those who might require specialized reading support. Most often this is an Oral Reading Fluency (ORF) screen where the student reads a one-minute passage and either summarizes the text or answers several questions. A good screen will take about 5 minutes per student. This allows a teacher to check fluency, accuracy, and text comprehension.

Diagnostic assessments identify the strengths and weaknesses of readers. They are extremely helpful for educators as they provide information regarding areas that can be addressed through explicit instruction. They include phonics word reading, vocabulary, and spelling assessments. The assessment you choose will depend on what you want to know about your students. For example, if you do a screen and the student is struggling to decode the words on the page, a phonics word reading assessment will pinpoint phonics concepts that the student does not understand or takes too long to decode. If spelling is a concern (even if they are reading well), a spelling assessment will help identify where more instruction and practice is required.

Progress monitoring tools do just what the name implies: they check for progress. Their use not only monitors growth with a standardized tool but, more importantly, they also help educators adjust instruction and strategies when growth is not occurring.

Summative assessments are administered at the end of the school year or the end of an instructional period to identify student achievement. They also help schools and teachers measure the effectiveness of their reading program/instruction.

> Recommended screens are listed on page 167.

What does this mean for the classroom teacher? If your district does not have a screening and assessment process in place, the starting place is a universal screen for everyone. This is not a benchmark assessment but a quick check for fluency, accuracy, and comprehension. If your district is using benchmark assessments, find an ORF screen appropriate for your grade level.

Once struggling readers have been identified, diagnostic assessments will help identify factors that might be hindering their reading growth.

If this feels overwhelming and you are not ready to tackle finding time to read with each of your students, try to find time to administer an ORF screen with your struggling readers.

If you are hesitant to engage in the screening process, I recommend starting with a spelling assessment. Although spelling falls under assessment, I see this as a universal screen. It can be done with the whole class and although it identifies those who are struggling, it also pinpoints which concepts you can address with the whole class (when more than 60 percent of the class does not have mastery of a concept) and what needs to be addressed with a small group (when only a few students struggle with a specific spelling concept). A spelling assessment will provide a snapshot of the skills of the whole class and guide you in choosing which lessons to teach from Chapter 4.

Remember that this work is a journey. If it is new, then choose one place to start. Once you see how valuable it is for you and your students, you can take further steps to build your skills and knowledge with screens and assessments.

The Why

Not only can you use screens/assessments to assess skills at the beginning of the school year, but you can also use them at several points throughout the year to ensure that instruction is supporting student growth, especially where there are lagging skills.

Assessment provides you with a deeper understanding of reading gaps and areas to address with explicit instruction. It supports scaffolding lessons within the classroom. Word choices, the amount and type of material used, as well as partnering and grouping for activities can be made more effective because of the knowledge assessments provide.

Screens and assessments are extremely important when creating small groups for targeted reading instruction within the classroom. When using only a benchmarking system, you may have two students at the same reading level, but that does not necessarily mean that they need the same targeted instruction to move forward.

If we think back to the Simple View of Reading, one student may need support with decoding, while the other student may need support with language comprehension. In any classroom, a teacher may have 4–5 students who are struggling with vowel teams, but they are all reading at different levels! By screening and assessing students, we will know what skills are not yet developed and can target those skills, regardless of the reading "level."

Screens/assessment can also go a long way if you have the benefit of working with a reading support teacher in your school. Approaching them with data and a knowledge of the skills that your students are missing (even though they have been explicitly taught and practiced) will help the reading support teacher plan targeted intervention more effectively. Screens/assessments are often the starting place for rich conversations with the reading support teacher, parents, and administrators. When school-wide, consistent screening takes place, it provides an overview of the needs and strengths of all students. It can guide class placement, intervention schedules, funding allocation and services, and school goals.

The What

Oral Reading Fluency (ORF): At the end of Grade 1, if students have "broken the code" and are decoding, ORF screens (that align with the phonics concepts being taught) can be implemented. There are several important takeaways from an ORF screen.

- It is a way to hear how fluently students read connected texts. Often this is measured in words correct per minute (reading rate).
- It allows you to check reading comprehension.
- It allows you to check word reading accuracy, as well as catch idiosyncrasies and nuances in student reading that might not be noticed in the classroom setting (e.g., dropped suffixes, mispronounced letter sounds, and students' strategies when approaching unknown words).
- It provides you with one-on-one time to listen to each student read.

Phonemic Awareness (PA): Since we know that PA is a reliable predictor of reading success in Grades K/1 (Kilpatrick, 2016), it is a critical assessment in the early grades. If students are struggling with PA, the sooner intervention begins, the more opportunity there is to build these critical skills.

As mentioned previously, you will probably not be doing PA assessments at this level, but in using the lessons provided in this book, you will be engaging in activities that target and strengthen PA skills.

Phonics and Word Reading Assessments: A good phonics or word reading assessment will provide lists of concept-based words (including nonsense words) for students to read. These lists are typically grouped by phonics pattern (e.g., vowel teams, VCe, inflected endings). Once phonics concepts have been taught and students are engaging with these concepts in print, these screens are incredibly valuable. They will show which concepts need explicit instruction (accuracy) and/or further review (automaticity). Some educators shy away from nonsense words, but if students can apply a phonics concept to a nonsense word, it indicates that the skill is fully understood.

Spelling Assessments: Decoding and encoding go hand in hand when it comes to reading instruction. When students spell correctly, it shows that they understand the structure of the English language. Spelling requires OM and letter retrieval skills. When students read, the letters are provided for them but when they spell, they must generate the correct letters, in the correct order, for each word.

> There are many excellent spelling assessments available (see resources listed on page 167).

Spelling assessment results will often align with the information gathered from phonics and word reading assessments, but not 100 percent of the time. Students who struggle with reading vowel teams will often have a difficult time using them in their writing. Spelling assessments will also catch readers who have strong decoding skills, but do not understand when and where to use certain phonetic patterns or rules. For example, a student may know that when reading, "ai" makes the long 'a' sound /A/, but when writing the word *airplane*, they are unsure whether to write airplane, airplain, airplan, airplein or airplayn. At this point, they often resort to their visual memory to decide what "looks right."

The key component of a spelling assessment is not that it indicates which words are spelled correctly, but that it focuses on the **types of errors** students are making. It should indicate which phonics concepts the student is struggling with, for example: errors with short vowels, vowel teams, complex consonants, inflected endings (e.g., *-ed*, *-ing*). With this information, you can teach explicitly to the gaps that show up on the assessment. Once the concept has been taught and practiced, reassessment can take place to check that students understand and use the concept correctly and with automaticity. One of the benefits of the spelling assessment is that you can administer it to the whole class at once.

The When

Since assessments and screens provide a snapshot of the skills that students have acquired, they can be used to create a baseline, especially if there is no access to previous data. Once an initial screen/assessment has been completed, you can teach targeted concepts and then reassess to see if concepts have been mastered.

Progress Monitoring: In intervention, screening/assessment and progress monitoring are integral to instruction, and this should be true in the classroom as well. If students are not understanding and applying the targeted instruction provided, it is critical to adjust instruction and activities. It does not make sense to screen/assess in the fall, teach all year, and rescreen in the spring only to discover that instruction throughout the year has not been effective. Although rescreening/assessment does not take place as often in the classroom setting, assessing several times throughout the year provides insight into how your students are responding to the instruction you are providing.

Although it sounds odd, there is a difference between monitoring progress and "progress monitoring." As a classroom teacher I want to know that students are mastering the concepts being taught because if not, I will need to spend more time working on these concepts. This may or may not include adjusting instruction, strategies, and time. I can observe how my students are responding to activities, have them engage in formative assessment to check for mastery, as well as reassessing with a standardized assessment tool.

In the MTSS model (and intervention work), a progress monitoring tool is administered at the beginning of the instructional period and then again at the end. This is a standardized tool and reassessing means using the same tool to measure growth. It may also be used at a mid-point in instruction to see if instruction is successful. After the initial assessment, goals are set, monitored, and evaluated at the end of the teaching period. These tools have been created for progress monitoring and can either be purchased or accessed for free online. They are different than summative assessment, mastery monitoring, and informal monitoring mentioned above. Of course, multiple screens/assessments over time are more insightful than a single screen/assessment since each screen/assessment only provides a snapshot of student skills.

"Progress Monitoring" is highly effective and well worth the time. It is an integral part of intervention and powerful at the classroom level as well. A full exploration and instructions in progress monitoring is beyond the scope of this book but there are those in your school or district that can either support you with this or point you in the right direction.

A Few Words about Intervention

For students with significant reading lags, it is important to realize that they will require more than classroom instruction to move forward. However, when classroom instruction aligns with intervention, students have the opportunity for more explicit instruction and more opportunities to practice their emerging skills. Although this book is about classroom instruction, there are ways to support struggling students in the classroom setting by aligning activities with their abilities. Sound-to-symbol word lists, alternative worksheets, and suggestions for scaffolding are included in the activities and lessons that follow.

As mentioned above, the classroom can be a difficult place for struggling readers to navigate due to years of failure and an awareness that they are not able to read as well as their peers. Every teacher who has taught these grades knows the damage that this has done, and is continuing to do, to student self-esteem. Dr. Steve Dykstra has done significant work in this area, and I highly recommend listening to podcasts or interviews where he talks about reading trauma created by our educational system.

If you have access to a Learning Support teacher at this age level, they likely have massive workloads. Any intervention you can do at the classroom level will greatly enhance instruction for students who need more support. Although there is limited time in the classroom, pulling small groups of students to a back table and working with them while their peers do independent work provides additional time and practice. If you have a quiet reading block in your schedule, this is a great time to work with struggling students. Even 15 minutes a day of targeted explicit instruction can yield results. Although students do not like to be viewed as different than their peers, students who have a trusting relationship with their teacher and see that they are making progress are often open to working for short periods of time either one-on-one or in a small group. This assumes that you can maximize this time with activities that meet students where they are and provide evidence-based skill building (which many struggling readers have not experienced with literacy). One place you can find evidence-based strategies to support these students is in Chapter 4 of a previous book I co-authored with Giancinti Alberti, *This Is How We Teach Reading... And It's Working* (2022).

When working with students, we always need to consider both **accuracy and automaticity** when they are learning and practicing skills. If they are not able to decode or spell as well as their peers, is it because they do not know how or they just need additional time and practice? There is no sense spending precious time on instruction if the student understands the concept being covered and simply needs practice.

Often struggling readers are already on the radar of Learning Support teachers. While there is often limited support for upper elementary/middle school students, it is important that they receive this help outside of the class literacy block. Removing students for support during literacy classes means they are not receiving extra time for instruction and practice. If these students remain in the classroom, and you can scaffold lessons based on their abilities, they receive exposure to new concepts and, as much as possible, the chance to practice and engage with the concept at their level. Push-in support, where someone comes into the classroom to support struggling readers during literacy blocks, robs these students of the opportunity for additional review and instruction.

This leads to the question of "When should students be pulled from the classroom?" For intervention to be effective and for students to move forward, they require 30 minutes, four times a week. Otherwise, reading support teachers are simply stabilizing the boat. If this time can be drawn from a variety of classes, students will not miss a large portion of any one subject. Gym, art, and music are not recommended times for pull out, as these subjects allow students a break from the rigor of academic classes, and these are often the subjects where they have a chance to shine. Rarely are schedules and support times ideal, but it is a noble goal to strive for.

Classroom Intervention Materials

It is important that, as you work with students above or below the reading skills of their grade level, they have access to the materials required. A trip to the library or the classroom of a colleague is often enough to access reading material that is above grade level, but it is not so simple for struggling readers in upper grades.

Decodable texts with characters and themes that are age appropriate are important. They do not need to be glossy, high-tech publications, but should contain topics that interest students and are at their skill level. Short texts or paragraphs without pictures avoid some of these challenges. There are now more systematic decodable texts available for older students on the market, and AI is becoming a viable tool for creating text that is accessible for all.

Fluency apps and technology programs where students are recorded while reading are engaging ways for students to practice reading and provide you with the opportunity to check recordings after school or later in the week. You can upload texts that are appropriate for each student and these recordings are excellent for tracking progress, sharing with parents (both concerns and successes), and using in e-portfolios and/or online reporting. Microsoft's Reading Progress is an example of this technology and is included in TEAMS.

One word of caution is that our most vulnerable learners need to work with our most skilled adults. Using fluency apps and programs should be for all students and is not to replace explicit reading instruction and support from the classroom or reading support teacher.

English as an Additional Dialect or Language

English Language Learners (ELLs) are a unique group of learners in our classrooms. When referring to the SVR, they need explicit instruction and support with both decoding and language comprehension. It is also important to keep in mind that each student comes to us with unique experiences with literacy, language(s), and formal schooling.

ELLs who began schooling in English in either Kindergarten or Grade 1 will hopefully have received explicit reading instructions along with their peers. In upper elementary, oral language **and** explicit literacy instruction should continue to be a focus of support. Some students will come with literacy skills in their first language, which will provide a literacy framework to work from when learning English. For others, especially students who have fled their home country and spent years in intermediary countries, there may be little or no reading and writing skills to build upon.

Refugees who have spent years moving from country to country before settling may have a smattering of educational experiences in several languages, which can be confusing. They may also come to their current classroom with negative experiences around school and literacy. Students I have worked with have shared that in intermediary countries they were ignored by their teacher or shamed in front of their peers. When this happens, it takes time to build trust and a positive attitude toward literacy.

Older students who have little experience with English will often need to start with letters and sounds, even if their home language uses the same alphabet. Since the Roman alphabet is not attached to all the same phonemes (sounds) in other languages, it must be explicitly taught. While it may seem "too young" to start with sounds and letters ("I don't want to take them back to grade one!"), it is important to look at it from a linguistic perspective. Share with students that this is the alphabet used for English, and these are the sounds that are attached to each letter. Instruction in the 44 English phonemes (depending on dialect) is important, as there are phonemes that are unique to English and the 44 found in English will not include all the phonemes of a student's home language.

If students come to school with literacy skills in their home language, it is important to encourage continued reading and writing growth in that language. Speaking with parents and ensuring that students have adequate and appropriate reading material for home reading not only supports developing readers but opens important literacy communication with parents. Immigrant services, inter-library loans, community centers, and mosques/temples/churches are all places to source appropriate books in a student's home language. Encouraging students to bring these books to school for reading periods or to share with their classmates creates opportunities for rich discussions about literacy, culture, and community. Many English-speaking students have never seen books that start from right to left, or texts in an alphabet other than their own.

ELLs will benefit from explicit instruction and practice with oral language and language comprehension, as well as decoding, with many opportunities to practice their developing skills.

Parents Reading to Students

Today's parents have busy, complex lives and many children come home tired after a long day at school. When there is minimal capacity to engage in explicit literacy work, reading aloud should not be overlooked. It is an excellent way for parents to support developing readers. Many students like to be read to and if reading aloud begins in the early grades, parents can move from reading picture books to chapter books to their children as they mature. As a Grade 5 teacher, I sent home recommended reading lists each year for both independent and shared reading.

Although books in hands is the preference for most educators, audiobooks are a great resource for students and families. Someone is reading aloud; they just aren't in the same room as the listener. For parents who do not read or read well, do not speak English or have other barriers to text, audiobooks are the perfect alternative.

> Sources for audiobooks can be found in the resource section on page 170.

There are multiple benefits that come from parents reading aloud to their children. They include:
- Exposing children to how written language is put together. Written language is different than the way we speak, and reading aloud helps children become familiar with its rhythms and structures.
- Helping children to develop a sustained attention in one direction. As children listen and engage with a story, they are developing stamina to pay attention for a sustained period of time. With the speed of technological devices, busy family lives, and a waning focus on conversation, children do not always have the opportunity to develop this skill in our current culture.
- Helping children to build vocabulary. A rich vocabulary enables children to recognize words in conversation, as well as in print when they are reading independently. Encourage parents to take time to pause and talk about new and unusual words when reading together.
- Providing exposure to new ideas, genres, and types of text. There is a body of research examining the link between declining empathy in children and declining engagement with story. As children read, or are read to, they enter others' lives, gaining access to their thoughts and feelings. This provides children with the big idea that not everyone feels the same way they do, or experiences events in the same way (Rymanowicz, 2017).

- Engaging in stories together. The physical act of sitting side-by-side with a book (or lying side-by-side listening to an audiobook) and sharing a story builds relationships. It contributes to the development of a positive attitude toward books and reading and it reveals the worlds contained within books and the pleasure and the anticipation of wondering 'what will happen next?'

Structure of this Resource

The chapters that follow typically share the following structure:

- Research and Pedagogy
- Activities
- Lessons
- Worksheets

The Research and Pedagogy section provides background knowledge and classroom application of the targeted concepts. Here you will find personal anecdotes, tips, and definitions as examples.

Activities require little set-up and can be integrated into your daily lessons. In some instances, activities also have worksheets. Where full lesson plans are provided, activities will be suggested to support the focus of the lesson. This may include worksheets for independent practice. To facilitate copying, we have moved worksheets, whether for an activity or lesson, to the end of each chapter.

Lesson Format

All lessons follow an explicit instruction model (Archer & Hughes, 2011) of I Do/ We Do/You Do:

I Do: The teacher introduces and models the concept.
We Do: The teacher and students engage in activities with the concept.
You Do: Once the teacher sees that there is understanding, students practice the concept independently with teacher monitoring.

The I Do/We Do/You Do model is not necessarily linear. You may introduce a concept and then practice it with your students only to realize that you need to do additional teaching and modeling (I Do). In another instance, students may be working on independent activities and you realize that additional instruction is required. You and the students would then move back to We Do until the concept is understood.

This method of instruction allows you to monitor progress and understanding and adjust instruction as needed, a hallmark of Structured Language and Literacy.

Pathways

Educators start where their students are (which will be evident through screening and assessment) and move forward from there. As you begin explicit instruction, some questions to consider might include the following:

- Are you concerned about the **vocabulary skills** of your students? Are you working with a significant number of language learners or students who have minimal vocabulary? If yes, then you might spend more time introducing and working with Tier 2 vocabulary. If not, you might need to spend minimal time in Chapter 3.
- Is **morphology** a new concept for your students? If yes, you might need to cover inflected endings before starting lessons in this book. If your students have already had instruction in morphology, they might be ready for the more complex affixes and Greek combining forms.
- Do your students know most of the **spelling** concepts listed in Chapter 4? Excellent, then just cover the ones where you are seeing gaps or weaknesses in their daily work and your spelling assessment. Does your spelling assessment show a wide range of errors? Then you may want to work through all lessons in Chapter 4, beginning with a review of digraphs and blends.
- If you feel you need to get right down to the business of **decoding**, you may choose to start in Chapter 5 with breaking apart multisyllable words and then teach missing concepts as you encounter them.
- Do your students need additional practice with a concept? If yes, take another week or two to practice and engage with the concept. Activities can be repeated using different words in the word lists. As well, different activities from various activity sections can be incorporated. This is a marathon, not a sprint, and you only have one leg of the race.
- If you know spelling and have spelling as part of your weekly routine, you may choose to start with spelling but begin to teach it explicitly, making sure that you are not working with words that have multiple phonics concepts that your students have not yet been taught. You can begin to embed morphology and vocabulary into your spelling program in an intentional way.
- If you do not do spelling because you know that traditionally it is just about memorizing words, you may feel more comfortable starting with vocabulary and morphology lessons (which might drive you back into explicit spelling).
- If you are reading this list and thinking, "Heather, my students need it all!" I do not recommend moving sequentially through the book. Instead, read the theory and background for vocabulary and choose one activity to start. At the same time, decide if you would like to start with morphology **or** spelling because they are too big to teach simultaneously when you are just starting on this journey. Teaching about affixes and bases in morphology takes time and so does starting explicit spelling lessons. Again, read the theory and background before starting lessons and activities. There is only one you and the goal is not to overload or overwhelm but to inspire!

It is a challenge to identify and address strengths and gaps in the upper elementary/middle school grades because students arrive in your classroom with a variety of skills, instructional experiences, and attitudes towards literacy. Know that there are multiple ways to begin using this resource and there is no wrong way to plan your instruction.

Summary

Bridging the Reading Gap is a starting place for busy upper elementary/middle school teachers. It is a look at some of the critical pieces that strengthen fluency, vocabulary, and spelling skills in older readers.

If this is all new for you, you can learn along with your students. The focus of the lessons shared in the following pages is **word play and exploration** and you are invited to explore and play along with your students. If you do not know an answer to a question, find out along with your students rather than feeling like you must be the expert in the room. Over time, you will become an expert, but it does take time.

If you are ready, dip your toe in the water and learn more about reading instruction that aligns with what researchers tell us about how the brain learns to read and the strategies that will support this work. *Bridging the Reading Gap* will provide you with many places to start.

Key Points

1. Teaching reading to students in Grades 4-8 involves addressing a wide range of skills, acknowledging a decline in reading abilities across grade levels, a necessary focus on content, gaps in teacher training, and shifts in culture.
2. Effective reading instruction begins with knowing students' strengths and gaps. Screens and assessments provide information about the students you work with. The Multi-Tiered System of Supports (MTSS) offers four types of assessment tools to do this work.
3. Research on how children and adults learn to read focuses on these components and instructional practices:
   - Decoding and language comprehension
   - Five pillars—phonemic awareness, phonics, vocabulary, fluency, comprehension
   - Orthographic mapping (OM)
4. Application of this research is Structured Language and Literacy (page 15). We continue to learn about evidence-based reading instruction and will continue to shift practices to align with new research.
5. Students whose reading lags significantly behind their peers can be helped by classroom instruction but some of these same students will need additional time and practice with a skilled reading interventionist. English Language Learners may also need support beyond what a classroom teacher can provide.
6. Effective parent support is as simple as reading to, and with, their children.
7. *Bridging the Reading Gap* is designed to be used in any order and in multiple ways. Concepts are organized by focus (vocabulary, morphology, spelling, and multisyllable decoding) and can and should be woven into daily classroom instruction based on your students' needs.

Vocabulary

"All words are pegs to hang ideas on" – Henry Ward Beecher, cited in Drysdale, 1887

Over my teaching career, I, like many of my peers, have been concerned about the decline in vocabulary knowledge, given the correlation between vocabulary knowledge and reading comprehension. Since vocabulary knowledge accounts for 50 to 60 percent variance in reading comprehension (Stahl & Nagy, 2006), it is well worth our time as educators.

> I was teaching a Grade 2 class online during the COVID 2020 shutdown and used the word "athlete." The teacher jumped in and suggested we talk about the meaning of the word. I was surprised, as I knew there were hockey players, soccer players, and dancers in the class. Sure enough, when we began talking about the word, students shared that they had heard the word but did not know what it meant.

Vocabulary is demonstrated through oral language (speaking and listening), reading, and writing, and it is a micro skill of comprehension. A lack of understanding of the meaning of words makes it difficult, and sometimes impossible, to understand a text's meaning.

Expressive vocabulary is a subset of receptive vocabulary, which is to say that students know more words than they use. Receptive and expressive vocabulary has implications for instruction, as more explicit teaching is required for words that are to be used in speaking and writing than for words that students simply need to recognize in text (Van Cleave, 2020).

Receptive Vocabulary: Words a person hears/reads and understands

Expressive Vocabulary: Words a person speaks or writes

As educators, how do we boost vocabulary knowledge and which words should we teach? These decisions are grounded in foundational knowledge about vocabulary that I wish I had known in the years I taught Grade 5.

The Learning Progression of Vocabulary

When teaching vocabulary, it is important that we understand the progression of learning a new word. You can find several versions of this progression but one of the simpler models consists of four stages.

Four-Stage Learning Progression

#1. We hear or read a word and we do not know what it means.
#2. We hear or read a word and it is familiar to us, but we do not know what it means.
#3. We hear or read a word and we know what it means.
#4. We use the word in speaking and writing.

#1 We hear or read a word and we do not know what it means.
When we look at this progression, we want to move right to #2 (the word is familiar) but we must honor #1, which is hearing or reading a word for the first time. One of our superpowers as educators is the ability to adjust our language to the humans in front of us. We are master communicators and want our students to understand what we are teaching and saying. While this is an important part of our role, we also must think of pushing vocabulary boundaries. Hearing a new word introduces it to a student's vocabulary and provides a pronunciation when they encounter it in text.

> I had a friend who taught Grade 1 for many years. One summer we talked about taking a trip to Europe. At one point she said, "Let's go to the Loovra." The Loovra? I had no idea what she was talking about and asked her to tell me more about this place. Her response was, "You know, the art museum in Paris." Ah, the Louvre. This is a highly intelligent, well-read educator. She knew what she was talking about as she had read a lot about the Louvre, she just had never heard the word spoken. Since she does not speak French, she struggled with the pronunciation. There are hilarious clips on social media of people reading books aloud where they do not know the pronunciation of names and places in the story and so replace the words with mumbles. It is not uncommon to stumble through words we do not know if we have no correct pronunciation to attach them to.

Reading aloud is a powerful way to expose our students to new vocabulary. There are many benefits of reading aloud to students, and one is exposure to new and unfamiliar words.

#2 We hear or read a word and it is familiar to us, but we do not know what it means.
Like exposure to a new word, this stage is also critical in expanding vocabulary. This is where we think that our work as educators begins. We want to support students as they learn more about words and help them develop an understanding of word meanings.

#3 We hear or read a word and we know what it means.
Once students are familiar with the meaning of words, a barrier in listening, reading, and accessing text is lifted. These words are included in a student's receptive vocabulary.

#4 We use the word in speaking and writing.
Use of new words in speech and writing (expressive vocabulary) demonstrates that students understand these words and have incorporated them into their

vocabulary. This does not mean that learning about a word is complete. The more students see and hear a word in context and the more ways they see and hear the word being used, the deeper the understanding (semantic lexicon) of that word and its word families (e.g., *accept* family includes *accepts, accepted, acceptance, acceptable*).

The Three Tiers of Vocabulary

If I had known about the three tiers of vocabulary (Beck et al., 2013) as an upper elementary teacher, it would have changed how I taught words. I thought my job was to teach new, content-specific words but it would have been more helpful to have taught the rich vocabulary students encounter in a variety of texts and across curriculums.

Words can be grouped into three tiers:

Tier 1

We use these words in everyday conversation that most children know and understand. Many Tier 1 words have Anglo-Saxon roots, which can make them difficult to spell. They are often called playground language. Examples of Tier 1 words include *car, house, man, bike, apple, run, fly*.

Tier 2

These words can be described as rich vocabulary that spans content areas and ideas. Examples of Tier 2 words include *contrast, approach, fortunate, benevolent*. Knowledge of these words provides access to a variety of texts and increases comprehension. Many Tier 2 words are derived from Latin and consist of a base and affixes. This means that morphology work (Chapter 4) will support exposure and understanding of Tier 2 words.

Tier 3

Tier 3 words are academic content or domain-specific vocabulary. They include words like *metamorphosis, rhombus, heterogeneous, isotope*, and of course *Louvre*! Students will usually only come across these words when learning, reading, or working within a specific area of study.

A Word About Basic Interpersonal Communication Skills (BICS) and Cognitive Academic Language Proficiency (CALP)

When working with English Language Learners, acquired language is often divided into two categories, Basic Interpersonal Communication Skills (BICS) and Cognitive Academic Language Proficiency (CALP). The terms are used to differentiate between the everyday language (BICS) that English Language Learners pick up on the playground and in the classroom as opposed to academic language (CALP) they learn in course work.

It is not uncommon for language learners to be viewed as proficient English speakers due to their strong BICS language, when in fact they may have CALP deficits due to a lack of time in school and academic learning in English. This is why we do not remove designations or codes for English Language Learners within their first 5 years of schooling; they have not had the time to be exposed to Tier 3 language.

Teaching Tier 2 Vocabulary

Knowledge of Tier 2 words helps students access meaning from a variety of texts across curriculums making them deserving of explicit instruction. The list of Tier 2 vocabulary is long and ever-changing as new words are created and others fall out of use. For example, if my students tell me an outrageous story I often laugh and tell them not to tell falsehoods. This is met with blank stares as *falsehood* is a Tier 2 word that has fallen out of use. Thirty years ago, if I told my grandma that the previous week had been full of *blursdays* (busy days that ran into each other) she would also have looked at me blankly as the term had not yet been coined.

There is no way that a classroom teacher, or a school system, can teach all the Tier 2 vocabulary that exists, nor is there a set list of Tier 2 words that must be taught, but we can work toward teaching as many as possible. In this way, we provide broad exposure to many words and an in-depth knowledge of some.

So, where does one start? First, I work with words that are encountered in text, conversation, and in the activities of the classroom. An awareness of the need to teach Tier 2 words will help you identify them as they arise. A second place to look for Tier 2 vocabulary is preselected lists like the General Service List (where Tier 2 vocabulary starts popping up in the 300s) and Academic Word Lists.

Head word example: *authority*
Related word forms: *authorities, authoritative, authorize*

The resource I turn to for Tier 2 vocabulary is the EAP Foundation Academic word list [Academic Word List (AWL) (eapfoundation.com)]. The list contains 570 word families that range from most to least commonly used in text. Word families consist of a head word and then words within the family. The 570 words are divided into 10 sub-lists and ordered in how frequently students encounter them in text. Each list contains 60 words except for list 10, which contains 30.

Looking at word families provides significant mileage in teaching vocabulary, and this is explored further in the morphology section of the book.

Not all Tier 2 words will be new to all students. While students come to us with a wide range of vocabulary knowledge, explicitly teaching and using new words is beneficial for all. For students who might know a word you are introducing and teaching, the repeated exposure you provide in a variety of contexts will deepen their understanding of that word.

Word Storage for Retrieval

The semantic lexicon acts like a mental dictionary of word meanings. This storage system holds information that we know about words besides the meanings (e.g., synonyms, antonyms, variety of usage), therefore our depth of knowledge about words, varies.

One important piece of vocabulary learning is ongoing use and review. Using new words in speaking, reading, and writing, and continual exposure to these

See pages 34 to 42 for related activities.

words, helps students solidify understanding and storage. If we introduce, explore, and then move on from new words, we minimize their retention.

Exposure to words in a variety of contexts is helpful, as is linking new words with known words. Think of the brain as a large filing system—if there is a file already in place, it is easier for students to make associations with a new word. For example, if a student is learning *sopping* and can link it to *wet*, *drenched*, and *soaked*, storage is more likely. The same is true of word opposites. Exploring words that are the opposite of sopping provides additional meaning about the word (e.g., the opposite of sopping is dry, arid, and possibly damp).

Learning Words in Context

Learning vocabulary in context is the most powerful way for students to see words at work and understand the variety of ways words can be used. You will notice that many of the activities below include context. If you are working with targeted words of your choosing, AI can be a helpful tool for generating text quickly. Although the quality of the text may be lackluster, it can provide a critical piece of vocabulary learning.

TEACHING TIP
Use AI to generate text quickly using target words.

Functional Vocabulary

Another aspect of vocabulary worth considering is the concept of functional vocabulary. These words, also called "connector words," are a micro skill of comprehension. If they are not understood, the meaning of a text or verbal instruction can be missed. For example, it is helpful for struggling readers to know when they encounter the word *because* the next phrase is going to explain what came before it. For example, "I need to get my hair cut *because* it is getting too difficult to manage."

> My favourite example of understanding functional vocabulary points the finger at me. How many of us have written test questions that ask students to *compare and contrast* two or more things? *Compare* means that one is to identify what is the same and what is different. *Contrast* means to identify what is different. If we want to ask students to identify what is the same and different, we just need to ask them to compare! Compare and contrast are both functional vocabulary words.

Functional Vocabulary Examples

Cause and Effect: because, so, therefore, thus, consequently, hence, since
Addition: and, also, too, as well as, moreover, further, furthermore, additionally
Sequencing: first, second, third…, finally, next, meanwhile, after, then, subsequently

---

> **Illustrating:** for example, such as, for instance, in the case of, as revealed by, illustrating
> **Comparing:** similarly, likewise, as with, like, equally, in the same way, despite this, in comparison, even though
> **Contrasting:** however, whereas, alternatively, instead of, unlike, otherwise, conversely
> **Qualifying:** but, however, although, unless, except, apart from, as long as
> **Emphasizing:** above all, in particular, especially, significantly, notably, in fact

Synonyms, Antonyms, Homonyms, Homophones, Homographs… and Heteronyms

Yikes! What are these and why are they often confused? An explanation of these terms is included here, and they show up in activities that follow because they support word storage (see Word Storage for Retrieval).

When it comes to synonyms, antonyms, homonyms, homophones, homographs, and heteronyms, we need to think word play. Rather than being frustrated, students should enjoy finding and using word pairs/groupings. Depending on the age and skill level of students, you will either need to introduce them one or two at a time or all together. Activities for both approaches are listed below.

Synonyms: Words with the same or similar meaning (e.g., sopping/drenched, shut/close, enormous/immense)

Antonyms: Words with opposite meanings (e.g., hot/cold, divide/unite, elderly/young)

Homonyms: Can be either a homophone or a homograph

Homophones: Words that sound the same but have different origins and meanings and may be spelled differently (e.g., piece/peace, heal/heal, there/they're/their); 'Phone' means sound/voice

Homographs: Words that are spelled the same but have multiple meanings (e.g., blue is a color, a sad feeling, a surprise 'out of the blue'); 'Homo' means one and 'graph' means to write

Heteronyms: These are a subset of homographs—words that are spelled the same, have different meanings, but sound different (e.g., read: "I will read a book," "I have read a book")

Complicated? Yes! What is important is the significant amount of word play that can be done with these words.

See page 47 to 54 for homograph, antonym/synonym, heteronym, and homophone activity worksheets.

Morphology

While there is a whole chapter of this book dedicated to morphology, it is listed here because morphology plays multiple roles in word building, reading, and comprehension.

The more knowledge a student has about a word's spelling, construction, and origins, the deeper the semantic lexicon, and therefore the more they are able to access its meaning. It can be as simple as knowing that *-ed* at the end of the word means that something has already happened (e.g., jumped, planted). Discerning meaning through morphology can also be more complex. For example, if the word is *portage*, a word that would be unfamiliar to many students, especially non-Canadian students, knowing that *port* means to carry would be helpful. If explorers had to stop and portage to get around some dangerous rapids, students would be more equipped to understand what is happening if they knew the word has something to do with carrying because it contains *port*.

Morphology is explored more comprehensively in Chapter 3 and includes a wide range of activities to support this work.

Idioms

Where do idioms fit in? They are not related to specific word meaning but they are unique ways of putting words together for new meanings and so they should be included here. They are tricky for English language learners and those for whom English is an additional dialect. Every language has idioms in one form or another so the concept might not be entirely new.

An idiom is a group of words that has been established by use to have a meaning that is not understood by the words that are used. In other words, it says one thing but means something else. Examples include, "it's raining cats and dogs," "pull up your socks," or "stop beating around the bush."

Exploring idioms can be highly engaging and students love them.

> One year I was teaching idioms to my Grade 5 students and asked them to write down as many idioms as they could find. I had a prize for the student who would bring in the most idioms. I absolutely **do not recommend** this activity! The next day I had notebooks on my desk with pages and pages of idioms. I did not have the time or will to go through every notebook and count them. I gave out multiple prizes for a 'job well done' and decided to never do it again. However, the engagement was high, and students got their families involved in the gathering of idioms.

There are two idiom activities included on pages 42 and 43. The first is an introduction to idioms and the second contains Greek idioms that have more complex origins. Again, the most important thing about teaching idioms is that students engage in word play since they can be challenging and often make no sense to students who are learning English or have limited vocabulary abilities. Idioms are important to teach so students are made aware that they are used in conversations and in text.

Oxymorons

Oxymorons are also a source of word play for upper elementary/middle school students. An oxymoron pairs two contradictory or opposite words as a figure of speech. The term oxymoron is an oxymoron as *oxy* come from the Greek word *oskús,* meaning sharp, and *moron* from the Greek word *morōs,* meaning dull!

Oxymorons can simply be two paired words like "jumbo shrimp" or a phrase like "the silence was deafening."

Additional examples of oxymorons include:

virtual reality	sweet sorrow	civil war	definite maybe
awfully good	crash-landing	good grief	ill health
lead balloon	paper towel	random order	unbiased opinion

Activities to Build Vocabulary Knowledge and Skills

1. Reading Aloud

Cunningham and Stanovich (1997, 1998) state that books embody more uncommon and content-rich words than any other medium of language, and the value of reading aloud to our students does not decrease as they get older.

There are many significant things that happen when we read aloud to students. From a vocabulary perspective, one of the most powerful is exposure to new words. Picture books and novels are full of rich vocabulary that our students will hear for the first time. When we read aloud, we often stop and explain words that we think our students might not know but need to access the text. Along with these words are those that do not directly impact a text's meaning but might be introduced for the first time.

Reading aloud also allows students to hear words in new contexts. This builds additional knowledge about a word and deepens understanding.

2. Passage Reading

Vocabulary learning is most effective when words are used and read in context. The big question is where to find texts when you have little to no budget. A few of my favourite places to find inexpensive or free materials include:

1. Jessica Toste (www.jessicatoste.com) and her team have created a free program called Word Connections. This multisyllabic word reading program is designed for older students and is full of short reading passages.
2. The Orton Gillingham Online Academy (https://ortongillinghamonlinetutor.com/) has great reading passages in their 'Developing Fluency' package. Newsletter recipients are offered inexpensive pricing several times a year.
3. ReadWorks (https://www.readworks.org/) has free texts available in a wide range of topics.
4. AI is getting better. You can use a variety of tools including Project Read's decodable text generator for struggling readers.

3. Focus on Stretching Vocabulary

As educators we are experts at adjusting our vocabulary for the audience before us. This is one of our superpowers as communicators: we choose and use words that we know our students will understand. To stretch vocabulary skills, we need to use words that our students do not understand but will help them access a variety of texts (Tier 2).

We should not be afraid that students are not ready or able to use complex vocabulary. If they can say *Tyrannosaurus rex,* name the Marvel characters, and all their favourite sports teams and players, then they can handle what we have to offer.

One way to do this is to pair new words with words our students already know. For example, I want to teach the Tier 2 word *consume* to my Grade 4 class. I can begin this process by saying things like, "We are going to consume our lunch and then go outside. We will eat our lunch before going outside."

"Once you consume your snack, be sure to clean up after yourself. Once it is eaten, put away the containers or throw out any trash."

"Before you water the cactus, check that all the water in the pot has been consumed. Make sure the cactus has used all the water before rewatering."

After several weeks of exposure to using the word 'consume' in this way, simply say, "We will consume lunch early because the field trip is this afternoon." and students will understand.

I am relaying information with the new word and then repeating the instructions with language that students understand. I am pairing the new Tier 2 word with Tier 1 words. There is a cognitive load on you when doing this work. You must choose words to introduce and then remember to use these words repeatedly so that they become familiar to students.

There are simple ways to slip in new vocabulary without having to remember to use new words repeatedly. Jen Nowell exemplifies this work with her check-in system. Each morning, students move a laminate owl with their name on it to indicate they are in attendance that day. Rather than using the headings "In" and "Out," she uses the terms "Present" and "Absent." Very quickly students learn these two Tier 2 words.

Courtesy of Jen Nowell

4. Power Words

One of the easiest ways to teach Tier 2 words is through story, because stories provide context for the words that are the focus of instruction. Picture books work exceptionally well since they are short and engaging. Although there are many fabulous picture books available for upper elementary and middle school students, do not overlook amusing story books written for younger students.

Before the Lesson: Choose a top-quality picture book that is not too long since you will be reading it 4 or 5 times. It might be related to content you are studying, address current events, reference historical issues, or explore social emotional concerns. There are many reasons to choose a text for these grade levels.

From that text, choose 4 to 6 Tier 2 words that students may not know well but that they will come across repeatedly in the text. Write the words on pieces of card stock.

Remember that this is about vocabulary and not spelling.

Day 1: Read the picture book to your students for pleasure. Nothing ruins a good story like someone teaching from a picture book before you have heard and enjoyed the story.

Day 2: Show the students the 4 to 6 words you have chosen and review their meaning. Explain that they are all in the book and that you will be pausing as you encounter each word. Ask students to either tap their desks or say "PW" for power word when they hear one of these words read aloud.

When students tap, stop as you encounter each word and talk briefly about the context and review the meaning of the word if necessary.

Day 3: Repeat the instructions from Day 2, discussing the words as needed. Each day, you can use a different short activity when encountering power words. For Day 3, students can turn and share with a partner another word with the same meaning.

Day 4: Reread the story and when encountering a power word, ask students to turn to a desk mate and use the word in a new sentence (unrelated to the situation and story in which it appears).

Day 5: Reread the story and when encountering a power word, ask students to turn and share with a partner a word or words with the opposite meaning.

Once the power words have been highlighted through 4 or 5 readings of the story, post the words in your classroom, and move on to a new book. If you read two picture books a month, you can teach approximately 75 Tier 2 words in a year in a very pleasurable way!

I have worked in classrooms where teachers have created some interesting power word bulletin boards. Chris Nowell has a Star Wars-themed power word board in his split Grade 3/4 classroom and uses the same color cards for words coming from the same book. One year Angela Pringle had a power word tree in her split Grade 5/6 room. Power words were popular in Angela's room, so the following year she created an ocean bulletin board and had the power words spill out of a treasure chest. The remainder of the bulletin board was used for other concepts being covered in class.

I worked in a school where multiple classrooms were using power words, so I asked the librarian to help us with book selection. She created two bins of power word books, one for Kindergarten to Grade 3 and one for Grades 4 to 7. As teachers used the books for power word lessons, they placed their chosen words on a Post-it® note at the beginning of the book. As the books were used by multiple classes, teachers did not have to go through each book finding power words since that work had been done for them by their colleagues.

Power Word Tree: Courtesy of Angela Pringle

Star Wars: Courtesy of Chris Nowell

5. Word/Speed Drawing

Drawing words may seem like a soft skill activity but if a student does not understand a word and its use, they will not be able to generate an accurate drawing. You will see word drawing as an activity in several of the spelling lessons in Chapter 4.

Words from books you are reading, content areas like science and social studies, spelling words, and thematic word groupings are all good sources for speed drawing.

This will become a student favourite!

Speed Drawing Instructions

1. Give students a blank 8 ½ × 11 piece of paper. Ask them to divide the page into the number of targeted words (usually 8). Instructions for dividing pages can be found on page 39. Students write a spelling word at the top of each box.

> You can create the page ahead of time and copy it. I recommend using prepared sheets the first few times you do this activity.

Activities to Build Vocabulary Knowledge and Skills 37

2. Before they begin, ask students to write their name on the back of the paper.
3. Set up a system of passing papers so that they rotate around the classroom. This may take a significant amount of time to teach and establish the first few times the game is played. I usually establish an order of passing. Repeat the instructions for the order of passing and then ask students to point to the person to whom they are passing. I check that all students are pointing in the correct direction before I begin the game.
4. Review the words, definitions, and drawings if needed. This type of modeling is more important the first few times the game is played.
5. Set a timer for 30 seconds and ask students to "begin." Students draw any word on the page. A time of 30 seconds works well for most students as it needs to be long enough for them to get something onto the page but not so long that drawings become overly detailed.
6. When the timer rings, students pass their paper to the next student. Once the new paper is received, the students choose any word on the page and begin drawing again (they do not have to wait for you to say begin). It is fine for them to draw a word more than once. If there is a blank space, students can draw that word. For students who struggle with reading or require support, stand near them and either make suggestions or read the words while the timer is going.
7. Each time the timer rings, reset it right away—students are expected to start drawing as soon as they receive a new paper.
8. This continues until all boxes are filled. Move through the class, supporting students as needed.
9. Once all boxes have been filled, students return their paper to the person whose name is on the back of the paper.
10. Students may do a gallery walk to see all the great ideas.
11. As a large group, discuss difficult words, words with multiple meanings, and why some words were left to the end of the game on almost every paper.

I usually introduce the game by telling students there is no "crying in the sink" (a great idiom), which means that this is a fun activity and there is no need to be upset or sad if their drawing is not perfect or they run out of time. Students love the activity, so this is not usually a problem. If students do run out of time, they can simply pass their paper without drawing or without completing their drawing.

Knowing your audience is critical for this activity. I once had a Grade 5 student who would not pass his paper because he did not want anyone to write on it. He became anxious, so we problem-solved the situation by allowing him to keep his own paper for the entire game. After several days of playing, he eventually began to pass his paper as he saw that other students were passing, and no one knows who creates each drawing.

Benefits of Word/Speed Drawing

1. You cannot draw a word if you do not know what it means. This activity will demonstrate word knowledge and allow you to push students to clarify word meaning.
2. Students become passionate about knowing a word and what it means.
3. Since students can draw any word at any time, students who do not have strong vocabulary skills can draw the same word over and over (if there is space) while having the opportunity to see what other students have drawn as papers are passed.
4. Students become free to draw because no one knows who drew which picture. Names are on the back and papers are passed quickly. This makes the activity safe for all students.
5. If you prepare the sheets in advance, the game takes 3–5 minutes to play. If students prepare the sheets, they get a bit of spelling exposure as they copy the words.
6. The creativity of students is impressive! You will laugh many times, and it will also provide you with some ah-ha moments as you get a glimpse of how your students think about words.
7. Students will beg for more of this activity.

How to Fold a Paper to Create Boxes

Have students practice folding the paper to create the appropriate number of sections. To make the task easier, share these directions that include the terms hamburger and hotdog folds.

- Hotdog fold: Fold a rectangular paper in half lengthwise.
- Hamburger fold: Fold a rectangular paper in half widthwise.

For 4 equal sections: fold hotdog and then hamburger.
For 8 sections: fold hotdog, hamburger and then hamburger.
For 16 sections: fold hotdog, hamburger, hamburger and then hamburger.

6. Connections

Connections is a word game where 16 words are placed on a 4 x 4 grid. The goal of the game is for players to select four groups of four words with a common theme or "connection." The New York Times has a daily game for adults as well as for kids. The kids' version allows players to choose between easy, medium, and difficult games.

New York Times adult version: https://www.nytimes.com/games/connections
New York Times kids' version: https://connectionsgame.org

This is a great activity to project on the board and play daily or fill in small segments of time while waiting for lunch, assemblies, or at the end of the day. Games

can also be downloaded and printed for a center activity or for independent work when students have completed assigned tasks.
Sample:

Word Grid

Monopoly	goblet	head	rod
basket	dog	Snakes and Ladders	Stanley®
tumbler	beach	golf	Checkers
cake	Catan	mug	volley

Answers:
Board games: Monopoly, Chess, Checkers, Catan
Things you drink from: goblet, tumbler, mug, Stanley®
Types of balls: volley, basket, golf, beach
Words that start with hot: dog, rod, cake, head

The game may contain terms or meanings that your students are not familiar with. From the sample, students might not be familiar with the terms *hothead* or *tumbler*. Since the goal is word play, exposure, and exploration, Connections helps students to not only learn new words and terms but also to think of common and unusual associations between words.

You can make your own games with the vocabulary you are teaching. For an extra stretch, you can have students create games and ask peers to play them.

7. Explain It to Me!

In this game, students generate definitions for Tier 2 words without using the target word in their definition. This is oral language work and does not necessarily require writing.

1. Divide students into groups of 2 to 4 or use it as an activity when several students have completed their work.
2. Project or write 10 to12 **Tier 2 words** on the board. You could also use **multisyllable words** with affixes to highlight morphology work (e.g., deconstructed—something that was built has been taken apart. The new fashion line includes a shirt that has been deconstructed.).
3. Students take turns choosing a word and making up a definition and sentence. They cannot use the target word in their definition.
4. Students continue taking turns until all the words are used.
5. You can extend this activity or create accountability by having students write their definitions and/or sentences in their notebooks/binders.

8. Anchor Charts

Create simple anchor charts in your classroom that focus on a single concept.

1. Post an 11x17 sheet of paper within student reach. In the center of the paper, write a Tier 1 word (e.g., wet).

2. Students suggest as many words as they can that describe *wet*: *sopping, drenched, damp, moist, soaked, saturated, soggy, dripping, flooded*, as examples.
3. A second method is to introduce the new word at the beginning of the week and have students generate the list as they encounter or think of words. You can even find a system for celebrating each time students use one of the words in speech or writing (e.g., points or a small privilege).
4. Extend this activity by asking students to place antonyms (opposites) at the bottom of the chart.

Over time you will have word charts posted around the room that are ready for writing inspiration.

9. Word Sorts

There are a variety of word sorts that can be created for vocabulary building. Although sorts can be done with a worksheet, using cards makes them multi-modal and much more engaging.

An example of a word sort might be using antonyms and synonyms. Provide cards or a word bank like the one below and ask students to sort the word pairs into the appropriate column. Don't forget to make "Antonym" and "Synonym" heading cards to identify what the students are sorting.

For suggestions on creating cards see Morphology Flashcards on page 77.

Antonym and Synonym Word Bank

after	before	bitter	borrow
chance	clean	considerate	correct
create	deep	delicious	despair
dirty	enter	exit	foolish
frequent	funny	goal	healthy
hilarious	hope	ill	intelligent
journey	lend	minor	opportunity
produce	purpose	seldom	shallow
smart	sweet	tasty	thick
thin	thoughtful	tomorrow	travel
true	wise	yesterday	youth

10. 'Wear a Word' Day (LETRS, 2019)

In this activity, students choose or are given a Tier 2 word to wear for a day.

1. Have a list of target Tier 2 words you would like your students to learn.
2. One or two days before the event, allow students to either choose a word from the list or give them a word.
3. Along with the word, students are given the definition.
4. The morning of the event, students write their word on a name tag or piece of painter's tape.
5. Throughout the day, students are encouraged to find out or ask about the words that their classmates are wearing.
6. This activity can be done orally, or students can be given the list of words and encouraged to write the meanings as they discover them.
7. Revise this activity by having staff wear the words, providing the whole school with an opportunity to learn a new set of Tier 2 words.

Activities to Build Vocabulary Knowledge and Skills

11. Vocabulary BINGO Review

Vocabulary BINGO cards can be created to review power words, curriculum content words, or words found in texts you are using. Using My Free Bingo Cards (https://myfreebingocards.com/bingo-card-generator), or Canva (https://www.canva.com/create/bingo-cards), create cards that either have the target word, the meaning, or an antonym/synonym of the target word.

Word Bingo: In this version of the game, read the word and ask students to find the meaning on their BINGO card. A bank of words can be placed at the bottom of the card to provide a visual of the spelling of target words.

Meaning Bingo: For more challenge, read the definition. Students then find the word on their BINGO card.

Antonym Bingo: Read the target word. Students then must find a word that means the opposite on their BINGO card. This can also be done with synonyms.

Idiom Bingo: Put the idioms on BINGO cards and read out the meanings. Have students mark the idiom that corresponds with the correct meaning.

This activity may spark an interesting discussion if you have words with similar meanings. Could one definition fit two words? These are excellent conversations to have and are as valuable as the activity itself.

12. Word of the Day

Dictionary.com has a word of the day that can be delivered right to your inbox. Each day there is a word, an image, the pronunciation, its origin, and meaning. It's great for English speakers as well as those learning English as an additional language.

Lessons

Lesson 1: Teaching Greek Idioms

I Do Begin by teaching idioms:
- An idiom is a phrase that has been established by their ongoing use, but their meaning cannot be determined by the words themselves. The word *idiom* comes from the Greek word *idios* meaning one's own or private. It is a fitting term as understanding an idiom is like a private joke for those who know what the phrase means.
- An example of an idiom is "pull up your socks." The meaning has nothing to do with socks or lifting. "Pull up your socks" means you must try harder.
- Using this idiom only makes sense if the listener is familiar with the term through frequent use and context, or if they know that "pull up your socks" comes from the British Army.
- The background to this idiom comes from when soldiers on duty would often sleep in their full uniform, including boots. When they awoke, the commanding officer would order soldiers to pull their socks up as this was the only task necessary to be fully dressed (Doughty, 2019). There are three possible origins for this term but this is the most school appropriate!
- Ask students to list as many idioms as they can think of. Students may not know the source of these terms, but they are fun to list and consider.

Possible suggestions might include:
- Under the weather
- The ball is in your court
- Break a leg
- Sit on the fence
- Through thick and thin
- Once in a blue moon
- Best thing since sliced bread
- Take it with a pinch of salt
- Come rain or shine
- Go down in flames
- See eye to eye
- Jump on the bandwagon
- By the skin of your teeth
- Beat around the bush
- Hit the sack
- Miss the boat

We Do Tell students that today you will be looking at idioms that have a Greek origin. Project the following idioms on the board or use the worksheet below.

Pandora's box	Achilles heel	Leave no stone unturned
Sour grapes	The wrong end of the stick	
Spill the beans	Between a rock and a hard place	

Listed below are the Greek stories that gave rise to these idioms. After you read each of these stories, ask students to guess the corresponding idiom. Be sure to number the stories as indicated here. If students are using their worksheets, they will place the story number next to the matching idiom. Once students have guessed correctly, share the meaning of the idiom today and use it in a sentence (these are provided for you at the end of each story).

STORY 1

This idiom means a weak or vulnerable point and it comes to us from a Trojan war hero. The River Styx was said to have great magical power and could make people indestructible. Thetis, a mother, dipped her child in the river by holding him upside down by his foot. This meant that the boy was protected except for the back of the foot, which was kept dry by his mother's hand.

In the Greek epic story *The Iliad*, Paris shoots a poison arrow which pierces the back of the foot of the hero. He is killed instantly.

Answer: Achilles heel—a weak or vulnerable point. "I have decided that I will watch less TV but talk shows are my Achilles heel."

STORY 2

In Homer's epic story, Odyssey was on his way back from Troy when he came to the narrow channel of Messina with dangers on both sides. On one side was the two-headed sea monster Charybdis (pronounced Karibdis), a sea goddess who lived under a small rock or dangerous whirlpool (depending on the version). On the other side was the six-headed sea goddess Scylla (pronounced Silla) who lived under a large rock. Odyssey decided to sail closest to Scylla and lost six of his men. If he had sailed close to Charybdis, all would have been lost.

Answer: Between a rock and a hard place—a dilemma where one has to choose between two difficult options (two evils). "I cannot decide whether to fly to Vancouver and pay the high-ticket price or drive and arrive late for the BC Lions game."

STORY 3

During the Persian wars against Greece, the Persian general Mardonius was defeated so he buried a significant amount of treasure. The Greeks searched and searched but could not find it, so they visited the oracle Pythia. Pythia advised him to search again, and they found the treasure.

Answer: Leave no stone unturned—check out all your options or all the possibilities. "When you are looking for the best price to buy a used mountain bike, leave no stone unturned." OR "Pythia told the Greeks to 'leave no stone unturned.'"

STORY 4

When the first mortal woman was created by the gods, she lived a peaceful life, not knowing about birth, death, evil, or hardships. That was all about to change. Zeus presented her with a box as a wedding present, but her husband told her not to open it because he knew what it contained. Unfortunately, she was too curious and while her husband slept, she opened the box, letting all the evils of the world loose.

Answer: Pandora's box—some things are best left alone, you don't know what you are getting yourself into, or don't let your curiosity get the better of you. "When she asked why his family had decided to move to Ottawa, he said that she should not open that Pandora's box."

STORY 5

Aesop was thought to be a Greek slave and storyteller. There are many stories attributed to him. One tale involves a fox and some fruit. The fox sees the beautiful fruit hanging from a tree and tries to get it. He is not able to reach the grapes, so he gives up and walks away, saying that it does not matter as the fruit was probably sour anyway.

Answer: Sour grapes: someone who doesn't get something they really want or who is jealous of something someone else managed to get, so they speak negatively about it. "When the captain of the losing basketball team said that the tournament was not a very important one, the winners said it was just sour grapes."

STORY 6

The secret voting system in ancient Greece involved a type of seed rather than paper. Voters put a white one in the pot to indicate a positive vote and a black one if they were against the idea being voted on. Voters had to be careful not to knock over the pot (by accident or on purpose) or the colors would be seen, and the secret would be out of who was winning the vote.

Answer: Spill the beans; tell a secret, either by accident or on purpose. "When Abdullah shared that the meeting was a surprise birthday party, he was embarrassed that he had spilled the beans.

STORY 7

In ancient Greece there was no such thing as toilet paper. In its place was a sponge or cloth tied to one end of a stick. This stick was used to wipe one's rear when required. If this seems gross to you, you will be shocked to hear that the sticks were kept in a bowl of salt water beside a hole in the ground (the toilet of the day) to be used by anyone who needed it. You had to be careful that you grabbed the correct end of the stick.

Answer: The wrong end of the stick—to misunderstand or misinterpret something or a bad deal. "We ordered a plate of nachos for the table, but the server got the wrong end of the stick and now we each have a plate of nachos."

You Do
- Have students work in groups of 2 to 3 to generate sentences using each of the idioms written on the board. This is a discussion activity at this point, and they should be able to create 2 to 3 sentences per idiom. Students can use the handout if they (and you) prefer.
- Once students have played with idioms and verbally created sentences, have them write their best sentence for each idiom in their notebooks/binders.

Additional Idioms with Meanings

Idiom	Meaning
It's raining cats and dogs	It's raining heavily
That's the way the ball bounces	Some things are out of our control
Hitting the books	Studying

Idiom	Meaning
Beat around the bush	When someone is avoiding speaking to you about something directly
When pigs fly	Never
Break a leg	Good luck

Lessons 45

Good things come to those who wait	Have patience	It costs an arm and a leg	It's expensive
By the skin of your teeth	Just barely pass	Barking up the wrong tree	Looking for the answer in the wrong place
A dime a dozen	Inexpensive and easy to obtain	A piece of cake	Easily achievable
Add insult to injury	Make something worse	Birds of a feather flock together	People spend time together with people who are like them
Flogging a dead horse	It is done and you need to move on	A bird in the hand is worth two in the bush	It is better to have something small and certain than something grander that may never happen
Under the weather	Ill or not feeling well	Bite off more than you can chew	Taking on more than you can handle
Know the ropes	Understand the job at hand	A red herring	Something to lead you astray
Read the riot act	Let people know what the rules are	The proof is in the pudding	The results will determine if something is a good idea or not
I've got it in the bag	I have this covered, I can do it	As mad as a hatter	A reference to the odd/crazy rabbit in Alice in Wonderland
The time is ripe	Now is the time to do it	Burning the midnight oil	Stay up late working on project
Break the ice or icebreaker	Get people talking or mixing	Handle with kid gloves	Be very sensitive
Make the grade	It is good enough, it meets criteria	Eye candy	Beautiful, good to look at
Turn a blind eye	When you pretend you do not see something	Play it by ear	Decide as you go along, do not make plans
The pot calling the kettle black	Someone who accuses another of something they do	A drop of the hat	To do something without delay
Jump on the bandwagon	Follow every popular fad or trend	Back to the drawing board	Go back to the beginning
Don't count your chickens before they hatch	Don't rely on something before it happens	Go down in flames	To fail dramatically

Worksheets

While these worksheets are ready for use, they also serve as models for creating worksheets with additional vocabulary words.

Working with Heteronyms

Heteronyms—words that are spelled the same but are pronounced differently (and have a different meaning)—can cause problems when reading. Identifying and working with these words will help with comprehension as students can try one pronunciation and then the other to find the meaning. To provide additional support, ELL and emergent readers can work in teams to complete worksheets they may find challenging to do on their own.

For the worksheet Quirky Heteronyms, we have included common heteronyms, but you can create a more challenging version of the worksheet by using the words *wound, bass, tear, subject, produce, attribute, console, content, object,* and *present*. We have included common heteronyms in the worksheet. Other heteronyms include *convict, object, invalid,* and *incense*.

Quirky Heteronyms Answer Key

- read (past and present)
- Polish (from Poland) and polish (verb meaning to make something shiny)
- close (adjective meaning nearby; verb meaning to shut)
- minute (noun meaning 60 seconds; adjective meaning very small)
- lead (verb meaning to go in front; noun meaning a heavy metal)
- bow (noun referring to a ribbon tied in a decorative way; verb meaning to bend reverently)

Heteronyms

Name: _____

Working in pairs or in groups of three, for each heteronym, write the two definitions and a sentence for each pronunciation.

read
Definition:
Sentence 1:
Sentence 2:

close
Definition:
Sentence 1:
Sentence 2:

lead
Definition:
Sentence 1:
Sentence 2:

dove
Definition:
Sentence 1:
Sentence 2:

minute
Definition:
Sentence 1:
Sentence 2:

permit
Definition:
Sentence 1:
Sentence 2:

attribute
Definition:
Sentence 1:
Sentence 2:

console
Definition:
Sentence 1:
Sentence 2:

Heteronyms (cont'd)

content
Definition:
Sentence 1:
Sentence 2:

object
Definition:
Sentence 1:
Sentence 2:

present
Definition:
Sentence 1:
Sentence 2:

produce
Definition:
Sentence 1:
Sentence 2:

subject
Definition:
Sentence 1:
Sentence 2:

tear
Definition:
Sentence 1:
Sentence 2:

wind
Definition:
Sentence 1:
Sentence 2:

wound
Definition:
Sentence 1:
Sentence 2:

Quirky Heteronyms

Name: _____

Each of the heteronym pairs below are spelled the same but are pronounced differently and have different meanings. Draw the meaning of each word and then write a sentence for each heteronym pair.

Sample Student Work, Wind

Challenge: Write a sentence for each pair of heteronyms using both words in the same sentence.

read	read	minute	minute
Polish	polish	lead	lead
close	close	bow	bow

Quirky Heteronyms (cont'd)

Sentences:

Heteronym pair: _____
_____
_____
_____

Heteronym pair: _____
_____
_____
_____

Heteronym pair: _____
_____
_____
_____

Heteronym pair: _____
_____
_____
_____

Heteronym pair: _____
_____
_____
_____

Heteronym pair: _____
_____
_____
_____

Homo"Phones" 1

Name: _____

Choose seven pairs of homophones from the bank below. Draw the meaning of each pair on a phone—the first one is done for you.

Homophone Word Bank			
ate/eight	bear/bare	break/brake	cell/sell
flower/flour	hair/hare	hear/here	no/know
male/mail	meet/meat	pare/pear	flee/flea
plain/plane	peace/piece	read/reed	sun/son
tail/tale	wait/weight	weak/week	see/sea

Homo"Phones" 2

Name: _____

Choose 7 pairs of homophones from the bank below. Draw their meaning on a phone—the first one is done for you. On the back of the worksheet, write three sentences that contain both homophone pairs.

Homophone Word Bank			
aloud/allowed	capital/capitol	ceiling/sealing	chord/cord
course/coarse	dye/die	fair/fare	grown/groan
holy/wholly	idle/idol	lesson/lessen	minor/miner
missed/mist	principle/principal	route/root	scene/seen
site/cite	slay/sleigh	sweet/suite	steal/steel
compliment/complement		stationary/stationery	vein/vane

Homophone-Homograph-Antonym-Synonym Sort

Name: _____

Sort the words in the word bank below into the appropriate column.
Homophone: sounds the same but have different meanings
Homographs: spelled the same but have different meanings
Synonyms: words with the same or similar meaning
Antonyms: words with opposite meanings

Homophone	Homograph	Antonym	Synonym

Word Bank

crooked/straight	bare/bear	brake/break	there/their/they're
admire/detest	accept/refuse	blue/blue	pair/pare/pear
night/knight	skip/skip	vertical/horizontal	approval/denial
quarantine/isolation	bow/bow	frequent/seldom	grate/great
comical/humorous	lead/lead	minute/minute	close/close
cruel/compassionate	train/train	novel/novel	sharp/blunt

Challenge pairs:

auspicious/fortuitous	obsolete/extinct
legitimate/authorized	wealthy/affluent
pacify/appease	intentional/involuntary

Choose one homograph and one homophone pairing and on the back of this worksheet, write sentences for each.
Challenge: Working with a partner, create sentences using as many pairs as you can in the same sentence. For example: During the **night**, the **knight rode** from the castle on the cobblestone **road**. Discuss your sentences before adding them to the back of your sheet.

Greek Idioms

Name: _____

As your teacher reads each Greek story, record its number beside the matching idiom.

_____ Between a rock and a hard place   _____ Achilles heel

_____ Pandora's box   _____ The short end of the stick

_____ Spill the beans   _____ Sour grapes

_____ Leave no stone unturned

Turn to a partner and create 2 or 3 sentences using each idiom (not writing at this point). Write the best of these sentences in the spaces below.

Pandora's box: _____

_____

Achilles heel: _____

_____

Between a rock and a hard place: _____

_____

The short end of the stick: _____

_____

Sour grapes: _____

_____

Leave no stone unturned: _____

_____

Morphology

My first introduction to morphology was a Pattan online workshop with William Van Cleave. I had a limited knowledge of morphology and found the presentation exciting and captivating. I saw immediately how the study of morphology would benefit both strong and struggling readers [as found in meta-analysis by Bowers and Kirby (2010)]. I signed up for a full-day online workshop with Van Cleave and it did not disappoint. As we were in lockdown during COVID, it was odd to sit in my living room and listen to Van Cleave as he sat in his.

So, what is morphology? **A morpheme is the smallest part of a word that has meaning**. This is not to be confused with phonemes which are the smallest units of sound in language. **Morphology, therefore, is the study of these small word parts.** Morphological awareness is understanding that words are made up of small word parts (morphemes) that have meaning.

Why Morphology?

Morphology is a strong predictor of reading ability, vocabulary knowledge (as referenced in the Vocabulary section), and comprehension (Nagy et al., 2006). Van Cleave (2020) states that if we help students develop morphological knowledge, it will help them build word sense, literacy skill, knowledge of content, and an understanding of multiple word meanings through the study of word families.

While this work should begin with emergent readers using common morphemes like inflected endings *-s*, *-ed*, and *-ing* (Moats, 2020), a deep dive into morphology can be done in later grades when readers are more proficient and have had more exposure to text and oral language.

Morphology is extremely helpful when it comes to breaking down multisyllable words. If students can recognize prefixes and suffixes, they will be able to separate them from the base word, making decoding easier.

While the study of morphology is complex, there are a few basic concepts that will provide a foundation from which to build.

Morphology with Latin-Derived Words

Latin derived words are composed of morphemes (word parts) called **bases** and **affixes**. There are two types of bases—**free bases** and **bound bases**.

A **free base** is a word part that holds the core meaning of a word and can stand alone. Examples of free bases are *cook*, *joy*, and *help*.

A **bound base** is also the core meaning portion of a word, but it cannot stand alone as an independent word. Examples of bound bases are *struct* (to build), *dict* (to say), and *ped(e)* (foot). These word parts need one or more affixes or another base to create a word (construct/structure, predict/dictator, centipede/pediatrist).

> **Free base:** a word part that holds the core meaning of a word and can stand alone as a word—help, joy
>
> **Bound base:** a word part that also holds the core meaning of a word but cannot stand alone—struct (to build), dict (to say)

The Difference between a Base and a Root

Many people ask what the difference is between a base and a root. Although this is a common question, it is not an easy one to answer.

A base and a root are slightly different. Both the base and the root refer to the part of the word that holds the meaning.

Root words…
- come from Latin or Greek origins
- usually are not words that can stand alone (bound base)
- can be referred to as a "word root"
- cannot be broken down further

Bases…
- can come from any language
- are assumed to stand alone but that is not always true (remember bound and free bases)
- free bases can have affixes
- cannot be broken down further

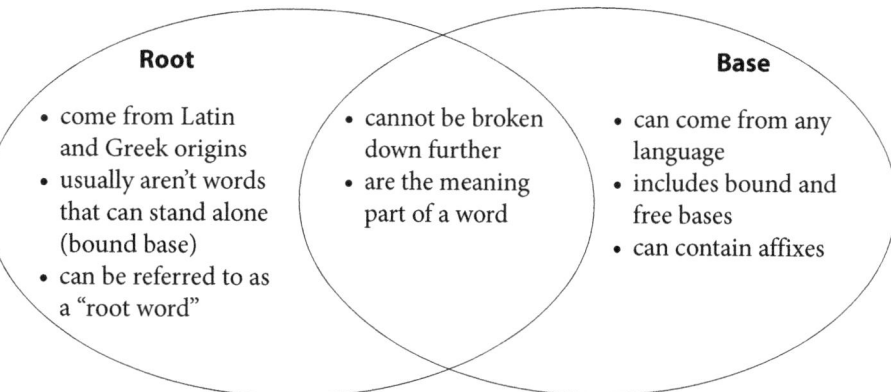

Relying on the wisdom of Willian Van Cleave, for the purposes of this book, **bases** will be referred to as the meaningful portion/s of a word.

Affixes

There are two types of affixes: **prefix and suffix**. If the affix is added **before the base**, it is a **prefix** and if it is added **after the base**, it is a **suffix**.

An affix adds to or manipulates the meaning part of a word and is attached (or 'fixed') to the base(s). They are important for comprehension as they tell the reader more about the meaning of the base word. For example, if the base is cook (add heat) but it has the affix *re-* attached to make it recook, it tells the reader that the food has already been cooked once and is being cooked, or heated, again.

You can add more than one prefix or suffix to a word (e.g., unhelpfully has one prefix (*un-*) but two suffixes *-ful* and *-ly*). Knowing the meaning of a prefix or suffix will not reveal the meaning of a word but knowing the base and seeing how the affixes impact that base is powerful and significantly impacts comprehension.

Suffix Superpowers
One of the important things to know about suffixes is that they can shift parts of speech. **Inflexed suffixes**, like *-ed* or *-s*, do *not* shift parts of speech but they can change how many and the tense of a word. For example, if the sentence is 'Where is the frog?' frog is the noun. In the sentence, 'Where are the frogs?' frogs remain the noun, there are just more of them.

Derivational suffixes like *-able*, *-ment*, and *-ful* change words from one part of speech to another. For example, to ship something is a verb, but a shipment is a noun—the thing being shipped. Identification of parts of speech (e.g., nouns, verbs, adjectives) can be taught through writing. This knowledge can then be applied when noting the impact of affixes on words and how they can shift parts of speech. This is deeper morphology work.

Assimilated Prefixes

Assimilated prefixes are something you will want to be aware of but are not addressed in the lessons in this book. Occasionally, a prefix will change its final letter according to the initial letter of the base to ease pronunciation.

Examples of assimilated prefixes include:
Ex- when added to *ject* drops the *x* to become *eject*
Ad- changes to *af-* when added to *fect* to become *affect*

Summary Chart

Term	Definition	Samples
Base: core part of the word that has meaning	**Free base:** stands alone	*cook*: to heat (re**cook**/**cook**ing) *joy*: happiness (en**joy**/**joy**ful) *help*: to aide (un**help**ful/**help**er)
	Bound base: requires an affix	*struct*: to build (con**struct**/**struct**ure) *dict*: to say (pre**dict**/**dict**ator) *ped(e)*: foot (centi**ped**e/**ped**iatrist)

Affix	**Prefix**: added before the base	**re**cite: to say again **pre**view: to watch ahead of time **un**wrap: to take off the outer cover
	Suffix: added after the base	teach**er**: one who teaches book**let**: a little book

Common Latin Affixes

Over half (approximately 55 percent) of the English words we use are of Latin origin (Van Cleave, 2020) so they are well worth exploring. The following prefixes and suffixes account for the most used affixes in English (White, Sowell & Yanagihara, 1989) and are ordered according to Manyak's suggested order of introduction for Grades 3–5 (Manyak, Baumann, & Manyak, 2018).

You will notice that common inflections -s, -es, -ed, and -ing are not included on the chart. Hopefully, these suffixes have been addressed before Grade 4 but may require review. I like to review -ed with older students due to the three different pronunciations (e.g., -ed—planted, 't'—jumped, and 'd'—played).

Prefixes	Meaning	Suffix	Meaning
dis-	not, opposite	*-er*	more of something
un-	not, opposite	*-est*	more of something, most
il-	not, opposite	*-er*	person who (English origin)
pre-	before	*-or*	person who (Latin origin)
over-	too much	*-ness*	state or quality of
mis-	bad, wrong	*-ly*	like, full of
re-	again, back	*-ful*	full of
im-	not, opposite	*-ism*	the act or state of
non-	not, opposite	*-ist*	person who
post-	after	*-ee*	person who
mid-	middle	*-less*	without
super-	over, extreme	*-able, -ible*	can be, worthy
under-	below, too little	*-ion, -tion*	action, result of
uni-	one	*-al, -ial*	condition, quality

mono-	one	-ity, -ty	condition of
bi-	two	-ment	the act of doing something or the result of the action
tri-	three	-ic	relating to
de-	take away from	-ous, -eous, -ious	qualities of
il-	not, opposite	-en	become
ir-	not, opposite	-ive, -tive, -ative, -itive	quality, nature of
inter-	between	-y	like
intra-	among	-ize	forms a verb from a noun or adjective
fore-	before, in front		
trans-	across		
sub-	under		
anti-	below		
counter-	against, opposite		
mal-	bad, wrong		
co-, con-	with, together		

The following are common Latin bases. Note that the list is not exhaustive by any stretch.

Latin Bases

Latin Base	Meaning	Sample
aud	hear	auditorium
cede	to yield	recede
circ	round	circumvent
course	run	concourse
crede	believe	credible
dic	say	discuss
gene	birth/origin	generation
ject	throw	project
jur	law	jury
manu	hand	manuscript

pede	foot	centipede
pend	hang	pendulum
port	carry	transport
rupt	break	disrupt
script/scribe	write	transcript
struct	build	construct
tract	pull or drag	tractor

Word Bank: Multisyllable Words with Affixes

Bases and Prefixes	Bases and suffixes	Bases with Prefixes and Affixes
misread mistake misuse nonsense nonstop overeat overrun overtake predict preface preregister subdue	durable illness lovable goodness possible sensible thankfulness valuable visible	misappropriate misprinted misunderstanding nonbeliever nonconforming nonproductive nontoxic nonverbal overprotective overseas prearranged predictable predominate prevention subversive

Greek Combining Forms

Words that come to us from Greek are organized a bit differently than those from Latin. The morphemes are not assigned specific roles like prefixes, suffixes, or bases. They can be combined with any base in flexible order and can also be combined with affixes. For example, the Greek combining form 'graph' can be used for autograph, biographical, and graphite.

The following list of Greek combining forms represents some of the more common forms, but there are many more.

Combining Form	Meaning	Example
anti*	against	antibody
anthro	human	anthropology
ast/aster	star	asteroid
auto*	self/same	automobile
biblo	book	bibliography

bio	life/organism	biography
chron	time	chronic
dyna	power	dynamic
geo	earth	geography
gram	written/record of	telegram
graph	to write	paragraph
hetero	different	heterogeneous
hydr	water	hydrant
hyper*	excessive	hyperactive
iod/old	resemble/in the shape of	trapezoid, humanoid
log	thought	logical
logue/log	to speak/speech	monologue
logy	study of	zoology
meter/metre	to measure	kilometer
micro*	small	microscope
mis/miso	hate	misogynist
mono*	one	monotone
neo	new	neonatal
pan	all	panoramic
path	feeling	empathy
pedo/ped	children	pediatric
phil/phile	have a strong love for	bibliophile
phobe/phobia	fear of	claustrophobia
phone	sound/speaker of/emit or receives sound	Francophone, telephone
phote/phos	light	phosphorous
poly	many	polygon
pseudo	false	pseudonym
psycho	spirit/soul	psychic
schem	plan	scheme
scope	viewing instrument	telescope
techno	art/science/skill	technology
thermo/therm	heat	thermos
tel/tele*	far off	teleport

*Commonly act as a prefix

Word Bank: Greek Combining Forms

antibacterial	empathy	polaroid
antibody	geography	polygamy
antidote	geological	polygon
antonym	geothermal	pseudonym
arachnophobia	germophobe	pseudoscience
asteroid	grammatical	rheumatoid
astrology	hyperactivity	subscription
autobiography	hyperventilate	sympathy
automatic	kilogram	tabloid
automation	microorganism	technology
bibliography	microscope	technophile
bibliophile	milligram	telegram
biology	monologue	telemarketing
biometric	monorail	telephone
chronological	neonatal	teleport
claustrophobia	pandemic	telescope
devoid	panorama	thermodynamic
dialogue	paragraph	thermometer
dynamite	phonetic	trapezoid
	phosphorous	

Shifting Syllable Stress

Stressed syllables may shift when an affix is added to a word (**per**fect-per**fec**tion, **cour**age-cour**a**geous). Teaching and practicing these syllable shifts models word decoding and students can try adjusting the stress syllables so their pronunciation of a word matches what they hear in speech (so it "sounds right"). Listening for and identifying the stressed syllables in words also supports understanding the use of schwa on unstressed syllables (p. 114). See activity 1 (p. 75) to practice changing stress syllables.

Connecting Vowel Letters

Since this is a book that introduces morphology, there are many concepts that will not be addressed through explicit instruction but are important, such as **connecting vowel letters**. Connecting vowel letters (sometimes referred to as connectives or connectors) are used when joining two morphemes to make the connection smoother (Linguistic Educator Exchange). They can be used when joining a base to a base (e.g., corn<u>u</u>copia), a base to an affix (e.g., fac<u>i</u>al) and an affix to an affix (e.g., malic<u>i</u>ous).

In Latin connecting vowel letters are 'i', 'e', and 'u'; in Greek it is 'o.'

It is helpful for students to think of them as glue because they are not morphemes. Examples include contin<u>u</u>al, phot<u>o</u>graphy, and fac<u>i</u>al. Just like when you add a suffix to a word, a connecting vowel letter will replace a final silent letter (e.g., phote – e + o = photograph). Unlike adding suffixes, it does not cause doubling (gram + o + phone = gramophone). Again, this would be a good next set of lessons after those listed below. In the activities that follow, and to the extent

Shifting Syllable Stress

possible, words with connecting vowel letters have been excluded for ease of instruction. However, it is important that you, the educator, are aware of them, because they will come up.

Seven Practices

We want to nurture readers, writers, **and thinkers,** so a problem-solving approach to morphology helps students build and retain morphological knowledge. Bowers and Kirby's meta-analysis (2010) identifies a "problem-solving" approach as essential to helping students apply their growing knowledge of morphology to actual vocabulary and comprehension instruction. These seven practices help to embed morphology in your everyday teaching.

1. It's All About Word Play

This cannot be said enough times! When approaching morphology, it is important to communicate and model that it is all about word play. It is not about memorizing lists of bases and affixes, and instruction will be powerful if students can create and deconstruct words with a sense of wonder and curiosity. You will find that even your struggling readers will engage in morphology work if it is exploratory, and they will be happy to discover that they do not have to deal with unusual spelling patterns found in Anglo-Saxon vocabulary words.

2. Spell the Affixes

When talking about affixes, **it is most helpful to spell** them rather than say them (Bowers & Kirby, 2010) since the affix may be pronounced differently according to the word. For example, the affix *-ate* is pronounced one way in *senate* and another way in *replicate*. The *re-* in *recover* is not pronounced the same way in the word *reply*. The reason, as mentioned above, is that the affix shifts the stressed vowel (**re**cover and re**ply**, **sen**ate and repli**cate**). For these reasons it is better to spell affixes rather than say them.

3. Embed Into Daily Practice

As you and your students grow in your knowledge of morphology, you can embed this work into all subject areas and daily conversations. As you encounter multisyllable and unusual words, you can pause and deconstruct them morphologically with your students. You can ask: What might this word mean? How would you break it apart? How do you know the meaning of the word? What are the clues? This application of knowledge will strengthen and support your students as readers and wordsmiths.

4. Spelling Over Pronunciation

Morphology is about meaningful word parts. Moats (2005), in "How spelling supports reading," states that meaning is more important than pronunciation when it comes to spelling. This can be helpful knowledge for students who drop letters when spelling because they are not heard when a word is spoken. As referenced earlier, there are also words where the same letter pattern can be pronounced more than one way. In the word pairs *heal/health*, *sign/signal*, and *please/pleasant*, the base is the same, but the pronunciation is different. There are also words that many of us internally pronounce differently when we are spelling. I know I internally pronounce the 'r' in February (Feb-ru-ary), the 'p' in raspberry (rasp-berry) and the 'science' in conscience (con-science) to help me write them correctly. Highlighting this with students can be helpful as they can identify the base when spelling, as well as support comprehension when reading.

5. Foundational Work with Suffixes

While prefixes can simply be added to the front of a base (except for a few assimilated prefixes), suffixes are not that simple. The ending of the base, the placement of the vowel in the base, and the first letter in the suffix can impact how the suffix is handled. In the lessons and activities that follow, the initial lessons address doubling the final consonant in a base and dealing with bases or suffixes that end in silent letters and 'y.' Starting with these lessons builds confidence when working with suffixes in subsequent lessons.

6. Examine Curriculum for Morphology Opportunities

When starting a new unit or in other curricular content, explicitly teach and play with the important bases required to support student learning. For example, if you are starting a chemistry unit, teach bases like sol (solute), homo/hetero (heterogeneous), and dil (diluted). In social studies, teach dict (dictator), gov (govern), and crat (bureaucrat). If it is color, teach chromo (chromatic), analogos (analogous), tertious (tertiary), and so on.

7. Have a Game Plan

Start by teaching the most common bases and affixes your students will encounter. Choose to work with a few affixes and/or bases at one time and then add more as students are ready. Many students are familiar with common affixes but have never stopped to consider what they mean. That is the work of explicit instruction.

Lessons

Unlike other chapters, we have placed the lessons in advance of the activities. Morphology work requires teaching bases and affixes before working with words. You will find that completing the lessons will enable students to engage with the activities with the necessary knowledge base.

Since we are exploring word parts, it is important to begin with how words are put together and how we take them apart when reading and spelling. The first two lessons address the why and how of adding suffixes to bases. While this is intuitive for many students, some students will need this to be explained. For all students, this work solidifies how English words are built and flexed.

Lesson 1: Bases and Affixes

Materials:
- Activities 2-5

Introduction:
Tell students that the next two lessons explore how words are put together. Many words have more than one part, and they will be looking at word parts and their meaning.

I Do
- Using the information above, explain and model that a **base** is the core meaning part of a word.
- Explain that there are bound bases and free bases. Share examples and have students come up with examples of both.
- Using this information, explain and model that an affix is a meaningful addition to a word that can come before or after the base.
- Affixes are
  - fixed, or stuck, to the beginning or end of a word
  - prefixes when added to the beginning of a word
  - suffixes when added to the end of a word
- There can be more than one prefix or suffix in a word.
- Words that come from Latin consistently use the base/affix structure.
- Talk briefly about Greek combining forms and how they are used to build words. Demonstrate the use of combining forms by using the word 'poly' and/or 'phone,' and as a class generate as many words as you can.

We Do
Write one word at a time on the board using the sample words. Begin to talk about the meanings of the affixes and bases as you look at each word. Have students guess the meaning of the word parts and identify the base (whether it is bound or free) and any affixes. Underline the base and circle the affixes. To support engagement, have students write the words in their notebooks/binders.

Free bases:
- unteachable (un=not, teach=to share information, able=it can be done)
- reporting (re=again, port=to carry, ing=an action)
- booklet (book=bound paper, let=little)
- unhappiness (un=not, happy=gladness, ness=a state of being)
- cooked (cook=add heat, ed=in the past)

- shipment (ship=to move, ment=changes the action (verb) to a thing (noun))

Bound bases:
- construct (con=with, struct=to build)
- migrate (migri=to move, ate=to leave)
- disrupt (dis=against, or not, rupt=to break)
- centipede (cent=100, pede=feet)

Together, generate as many words as possible using the Greek combining forms below.
- bio (life/organism)
- auto (self/same)
- graph (to write)
- tel/tele (far off)

You Do **Choose from the following activities:**
1. Select from activities on pages 75–76.
2. Drawing from the word banks on pages 70 and 73 or using your own list of words, provide students with additional words to independently identify the base and affixes. Review together at the end of class.
3. Have students generate their own multisyllable words with a base and affixes. For each word, they are to underline the base and circle the affixes.

Lesson 2: The Doubling Rule

Introduction
Tell students that this week you will be learning when to double and when not to double the final letter in a word before adding an affix. Note that the following lesson addresses when a base needs to be altered by dropping or changing the final letter (e.g., happy to happiest).

I Do Review the Doubling Rule

No: Do not double if the:
- suffix begins with a consonant (e.g., flat**n**ess, dim**n**ess)
- base word ends in two consonants (e.g., re**nt**er, cli**mb**ing, ju**mp**ed)
- base word contains two vowels (e.g., sw**oo**ped, f**ee**ling, l**oo**ter)

Yes: Double if the:
- suffix begins with a vowel (e.g., pa**tt**ing, bi**gg**est, ste**pp**ed)
- base word is one syllable (e.g., **clip**ping, **fan**ned, **bat**ter)
- word ends in one consonant preceded by one vowel (e.g., **nut**ty, **dot**ted, **star**red)

"No" trumps "yes" every time!
For example, *rent* is one syllable, it has one vowel and the suffix *-ing* starts with a vowel but… there are two consonants before the suffix, so you do not double the 't.'

Lessons 67

We Do On the board demonstrate how the final consonant is doubled in the words listed below. Have students write the words in their notebooks/binders as you work through them together.

Words we double the final consonant:

big: bigger, biggest clip: clipped, clipping, clipper
dot: dotted, dotting drag: dragged, dragging
fat: fatter, fattest step: stepping, stepped
star: starred, starring flat: flatter, flattest
hot: hotter, hottest sin: sinned, sinning, sinner

Words we don't double the final consonant:
If the base word ends in 2 consonants:

faster, fastest renter, renting
brushing, brushed farmer, farmed, farming
perched, perching charming, charmed, charmer
sorter, sorting, sorted

If the suffix begins with a consonant:

flatness, flatly hotly, hotness
sinful

If the base word ends in 2 consonants:

faster, fastest renter, renting
brushing, brushed farmer, farmed, farming
perched, perching charming, charmed, charmer
sorter, sorting, sorted

If the base word has 2 vowels:

swooped, swooping boiling, boiled, boiler
aimer, aiming, aimed cheated, cheating, cheater
needed, needing, needy toaster, toasted, toasting
cloudy, clouded draining, drained
steamy, steamer spoiler, spoiled, spoiling
roofer, roofing, roofed groaner, groaning, groaned
counter, counting

You Do
- Worksheet "The Doubling Rule" (page 74)
- Review the affixes before or as you work through the sheet if you are doing it as a class. These will be reviewed again in later lessons as this is an introduction to suffixes.
  - *-er*: the person who does it or more
  - *-ed*: has already happened
  - *-est*: the most
  - *-ing*: is happening now
  - *-ment*: the act of doing something or the result of the action turns a verb to a noun (action to thing) ship is to move = shipment is the thing that is moved
  - *-ly*: turns an adjective into an adverb (describes the verb)

Review the worksheet as a class.

Lesson 3: Adding Suffixes to Words that End in 'e'

There are a few guidelines that will support students when they are adding a suffix to a word that ends in 'y' or a silent 'e.' Teaching this lesson before working with these words will provide knowledge that students can rely on when building and disassembling words.

Words that End in a Silent 'e'
When adding a suffix to words that end in silent 'e,' the silent 'e' is dropped when adding a suffix that starts with a vowel. For example:

hop**e** + ed = hoped   gat**e** + ed = gated
excit**e** + able = excitable   gam**e** + ing = gaming
fam**e** + ous = famous   lik**e** + able = likable

Hope is a good example to use because this demonstrates why we use the doubling rule. If we did not double the 'p' in *hop* to make *hopping*, we would have the word *hoping*.

Sometimes students will think that if the word ends in silent 'e' and a suffix like *-ed* starts with an 'e,' they simply add a 'd,' but this is not so. The silent 'e' is dropped and the suffix *-ed* is added.

If a word ends in a silent 'e' and the suffix starts with a consonant, then the silent 'e' is retained.

hop**e** + less = hopeless   gat**e** + less = gateless
lik**e** + ly = likely   excit**e** + ment = excitement

Exceptions
When 'e' follows 'c' or 'g' at the end of a word creating a soft 'g' or 'c' sound (lesson page 129), the 'e' must be retained when adding a suffix. If the suffix begins with an 'e,' 'i,' or 'y,' the 'e' can be dropped as these three vowels all create the soft 'c' and 'g' sound. However, if the suffix starts with 'a,' 'o,' or a consonant, the 'e' must be retained. For example: *change* to *changing/changeable*, *strange* to *stranger/strangeness*, *judge* to *judging* and *judgeable*, and *glance* to *glancing/glanced*.

I Do — Using the information above, explain and model adding a suffix to words that end in 'e.'

- If the suffix begins with a consonant, retain the silent 'e.'
- If the suffix begins with a vowel, drop the silent 'e' and add the suffix.
- If the word ends in 'ce' or 'ge,' the soft 'c' and 'g' sound must be maintained. If the suffix begins with 'e,' 'i,' or 'y,' drop the silent 'e.' If the suffix begins with 'a' or 'o,' retain the silent 'e' and add the suffix.
- Model these concepts using the sample words above.

We Do
- Using the following word list, or words you are working with in class, model adding suffixes to words that end in silent 'e.'
- Have students write the words in their notebooks/binders.
- Using the word list below, play games like **Is It Spelled Correctly?** and **It's Up to You** (pages 106–107).

You Do
- Provide students with a list of words that end in silent 'e' and a selection of suffixes that start with vowels and consonants. You can use the word bank

below or words you are working with in class and the suffix list on page 73. Suggested suffixes might include *-ment, -ing, -ed, -est, -ly, -ful, -ness, -able, -y, -er,* and *-less*.
- Ask students to generate words in their notebooks/binders.
- **Extending:** Have students create sentences using as many target words as possible in one sentence (and still have the sentence make sense).

Words that end in 'e'			
Tier 1	**Tier 2**	**Do not drop the 'e'**	
bake	assemble	acknowledge	gauge
brave	blare	age	gouge
excite	calculate	allege	grace
have	debate	barge	hence
late	desire	begrudge	judge
like	dine	brace	knowledge
loose	extreme	budge	mile
love	fate	change	mince
make	lease	courage	notice
move	prove	cringe	nudge
paddle	state	fence	peace
promise	subdue	force	verge
size	unique		
time	value		
wise	waste		
	whine		

Exceptions
Retain the 'e' when the suffix begins with a vowel:
dye — dyeing   shoe — shoeing   toe — toeing

Drop the 'e' when the suffix begins with a consonant:
due — duly   subtle — subtly   true — truly   whole — wholly

Lesson 4: Adding Suffixes to Words that End in 'Y'

When adding a suffix to words that end in 'y,' one must look at what letter comes before the 'y.' Different rules are at play if the letter before the 'y' is a vowel or a consonant.

When a word ends in vowel-y:
When single and multisyllable words end in **vowel-y**, the 'y' is not dropped before the suffix is added because the 'y' is part of a vowel team (e.g., boy, monkey, betray).

stay + ing = staying   grey + er = greyer

When a word ends in consonant-y:
When single and multisyllable words end in **consonant-y**, the 'y' is not dropped but changed to an 'i' before the suffix is added. For example, the word *comply* has a consonant before the final 'y.' When you add *-ed* to *comply*, you must change the 'y' to an 'i' and add 'ed': *complied*. This rule applies whether the suffix starts with a vowel or a consonant.

dry + est = driest
cry + ed = cried
sunny + est = sunniest

carry + er = carrier
comply + ed = complied

Exceptions for Changing 'y' to 'i'

Creating plurals when words end in 'y'
There is an exception to the "change 'y' to an 'i' rule when adding 's' to a word that ends in consonant-y. The exception occurs when making it plural. In this case, the 'y' is changed to an 'i' but an 'es' is always used (rather than the common 's'). Examples include:

bunny + es = bunnies
city + es = cities

puppy + es = puppies
balcony + es = balconies

Creating plurals for words that end in vowel-y follow the traditional pattern of simply adding an 's.' Examples include:

monkey + s = monkeys
delay + s = delays

journey + s = journeys
play + s = plays

Suffixes that start with 'i'
When a suffix begins with an 'i' (e.g., *-ing* or *-ish*) the 'y' is retained because no English words have a double 'i.'

pry + ing = prying
dirty + ish = dirtyish

apply + ing = applying
noisy + ish = noisyish

Changing 'i' to an 'y'
There is a quirky instance when we do the opposite and change the 'i' to a 'y,' after dropping the silent 'e.' For example:

die + ing = dying

lie + y = lying

To complicate matters further, if we are talking about coloring fabric – to dye, the 'e' must be retained (dyeing) so that it is not confused with the end of life.

Changing 'y' to 'i' when words end in 'ay'
Some **ay** words change the vowel team from 'ay' to 'ai' and then add a suffix. When this happens, the suffixes are sometimes adjusted as well (e.g., when pay changes to paid the 'e' is dropped from 'ed').

day + ly = da**i**ly
gay + ety = ga**i**ety. Also, gaily
lay – laid
pay – paid
say – said
slay – slain

Reading words where the 'y' has changed to an 'i'
The sound of 'y' in the base word is usually retained when a suffix is added. For example, in the words *carry* and *carried*, the 'y' makes a long 'e' (/E/) sound. In the words *fry* and *fryer*, the 'y' makes the long 'i' (/I/) sound. There are a few exceptions to this rule which students will often naturally flex because they have heard and used these words in speech (e.g., easy/easily, happy/happily).

So many exceptions!!!

This really is a tricky concept because there are so many exceptions. It is important that the focus remains on play and experimentation, rather than memorizing lists of rules. These exceptions are listed so that you, the teacher, can navigate some of the questions you will be asked.

Adding Suffixes to words that end in 'y'

I Do Using the information provided above review the rules for adding suffixes when words end in 'y.' I would introduce the concept without going into all exceptions at this point.

- When words end in **vowel-y**, the 'y' is not dropped before the suffix is added because the 'y' is part of a vowel team (e.g., boy, monkey, betray).
  stay + ing = staying   grey + er = greyer
- When words end in **consonant-y**, the 'y' is not dropped but changed to an 'i' before the suffix is added.
  dry + est = driest   carry + er = carrier
- If the word ends in consonant-y and the suffix starts with a vowel, retain the 'y.'

We Do
1. Using the word list below, or words you are working with in class, model adding suffixes to words that end in 'y.'
2. Have students write the words in their notebooks/binders.
3. Using the word list below, play games like **Is It Spelled Correctly?** and **It's Up to You** (pages 106–107).
4. Teach the exception of adding 's' to words that end in 'y.' Write the word on the board and model adding 's' and 'es.' Have students write these in their binders/notebooks.
5. Teach the exception of adding suffixes that start with 'i' to words that end in 'y.' Write the words on the board and model adding suffixes that start with '-*ing*.' Have students write these in their binders/notebooks.

You Do
- Provide students with a list of words that end in 'y' and a selection of suffixes that start with vowels and consonants. You can use the word bank below or words you are working with in class and the suffix list on page 73. Suggested suffixes might include -*ment*, -*ing*, -*ed*, -*est*, -*ly*, -*ful*, -*ness*, -*able*, -*y*, -*er*, and -*less*.
- Ask students to generate words in their notebooks/binders.
- **Extending:** Have students create sentences using as many words as possible in one sentence (and still make sense).

Word Bank: Adding suffixes to words that end in 'y'			
Change 'y' to an 'i'		**Retain the 'y'**	
Tier 1	Tier 2	Tier 1	Tier 2
angry	apply	delay	betray
beauty	balcony	enjoy	buoy
busy	bawdy	grey	coy
cozy	ceremony	joy	decay
dirty	defy	key	deploy
early	deny	monkey	foray
easy	downy	obey	journey
empty	draughty	ordinary	ploy
greedy	droopy	play	portray
happy	edgy	turkey	prey
hazy	employ	valley	relay
lazy	frisky		slay
lucky	gangly		splay
nasty	lonely		stray
noisy	magnify		
pity	mercy		
ready	moody		
sandy	orderly		
silly	rally		
stormy	rely		
sunny	spicy		
tasty	spry		
tiny	supply		
	treaty		
	wary		
	wry		

Lessons

The Doubling Rule

Name : _____

Add the suffix -*er* (person who does it or more) to the following words:

big _____   clip _____

farm _____   moan _____

Add the suffix -*est* (most) to the following words:

quick _____   fast _____

flat _____   neat _____

Add the suffix -*ment* (the act of doing something or the result of the action) to the following words:

ship _____   enjoy _____

enchant _____   appoint _____

Add the suffix -*ed* (already happened) to the following words:

star _____   toast _____

perch _____   need _____

Add the suffix -*ly* (like, full of) to the following words:

flat _____   short _____

sweet _____   hot _____

Add the suffix -*ing* (happening now) to the following words:

brush _____   star _____

groan _____   shop _____

Next Steps in Morphology

The activities and lessons in this chapter are a starting place for studying morphology with your students. If you would like to work further with morphology, instruction in how affixes impact parts of speech and working with connecting vowel letters would be where I would look next.

Activities

Many of the activities in this section are created with specific bases, affixes, and Greek combining forms. All can be adjusted for the bases and affixes you are working on in class. **Use the concept and create more activities using different bases, affixes, and Greek combining forms.** Note that the activity descriptions below are followed by individual worksheet pages that support these foci.

1. Shifting Syllable Stress

Reading lists of word pairs like **univer**se to uni**ver**sity, **ath**lete to ath**let**ic, and **cour**age to cou**rage**ous draws awareness to stressed syllables and how they shift when an affix is added to a word. Teaching and practicing these syllable shifts models word decoding. Students can try adjusting the stressed syllables so their pronunciation of a word matches what they hear in speech (so it "sounds right"). Listening for and identifying stressed syllables in words also supports understanding the use of schwa in unstressed syllables (p. 114). Extend this word pair reading activity by asking students to find or share words where the vowel stress shifts with the addition of an affix.

You can also display and read the following list of words together and note the change in syllable emphasis.

episode – epi**sod**ic
telepath – tele**path**y
biography – bio**graph**ic
athlete – ath**let**ic
universe – uni**ver**sity
re**cov**er – re**cov**ery
import – im**port**ant
con**trib**ute – con**trib**ution
music – mu**si**cian
perfect – per**fec**tion

contest – con**test**ant
courage – cou**rage**ous
captive – cap**tiv**ity
finite – in**fin**ity
photograph – pho**tog**raphy
ac**com**modate – accommo**da**tion
ad**van**tage – advan**ta**geous
proverb – pro**verb**ial
drama – dra**mat**ic
situate – situ**a**tion

2. Exploding Bases and Greek Combining Forms

In this activity, students identify the base in a word and then think of as many words as they can that also contain that base (see the worksheet on page 82). You can have your students work in pairs for the added benefit of having them orally generate words and discuss whether they are real or not and what they might mean. Extend this activity by having students create sentences with their words. Again, embed oral language skills by having students work in pairs or groups of three to generate sentences and then record their best sentences in their notebooks/binders or on the back of their worksheet.

3. Base and Affix Sorting

There are several worksheets that follow that focus on base and affix sorting. You can use these or create your own worksheet to align with affixes and bases you have been explicitly teaching. Note that for some activities the same word can be used in multiple spots. Embed oral language skills by having students work in pairs or groups of three to generate sentences and then record their best sentences in their notebooks/binders or on the back of their worksheets.

4. Affix Addition

As a class, take a base or Greek combining form and create as many words as you can by adding affixes. It can be a simple word, such as *teach* or more complex, such as *port*. For example:

teach: reteach, teaching, teacher, teachable, preteach
port: report, support, transport, export, import, deport

Have students work in pairs or groups of three to orally generate a sentence for each word. They can write their best sentences in their notebooks/binders.

5. Student Built Matrices

Introduce this activity by having students generate words from the matrix for *heat*. Show them that with this matrix they can make the words *reheat*, *preheat*, *unheat*, *heater*, *heatable*, *heating*, and so on.

re-	heat –to increase temperature	-er
pre-		-able
un-		-ing

Once students understand the concept, have them make their own matrices using the worksheets on pages 87–90. The first worksheet has simple bases and Greek combining forms whereas the second worksheet is more challenging.

6. Creating Words with a Matrix

There are many, many matrices online. Simply google word matrix under images and a wealth of options will appear. You can also create your own matrices by using this free tool by Neil Ramsden: http://www.neilramsden.co.uk/spelling/matrix/run.html?version=temp

Before using the related worksheet on page 87, project a matrix onto the board and either work on generating words as a class, or have students work in their notebooks/binders to create as many words as possible. This is a great activity for when you have a bit of time to fill. If you have the matrices stored in a digital file, you can pull them up and project them at any time.

7. Interactive Morphology Bulletin Boards and Pocket Charts

A great way to allow students to play and engage with affixes and bases is to create interactive bulletin boards or pocket charts using cards (or Post-it® notes for the bulletin board). Students and teachers can move bases, affixes, and Greek combining forms to create words. There are many pictures online. The pocket chart example below is from This Reading Mama (Morphology Pocket Chart Cards - This Reading Mama).

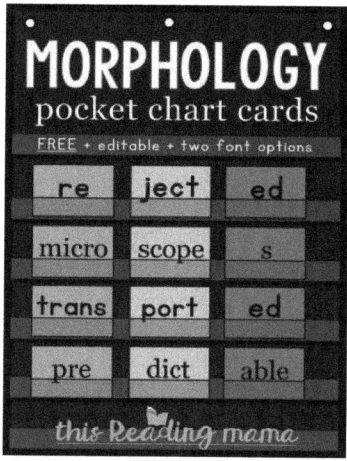

Courtesy of Becky Spence

8. Oral Morpheme Manipulation

This is one of Van Cleave's brilliant ideas. Start with a simple single or multisyllable word and ask students for suggestions for adding, subtracting, or substituting one morpheme at a time.

For example:

- Provide the word *teach*.
- Ask students to add a suffix. They suggest *-ing* to create teaching.
- Ask students to change the *-ing* to something new. Students suggest *teachable*.
- Ask students to add a prefix to teachable. Students suggest *unteachable*.
- Ask students to replace the base. Students suggest *think* for *unthinkable*.
- Ask students to replace the prefix. Can they do it?
- Once students are stumped, begin again with another base or combining form.
- This can become an independent activity if students write the initial word in their notebooks/binders and then respond to each prompt in writing. At the end of the game, see how many different words students have created considering they all started with the same initial word.

9. Morphology Flashcards

There are many flashcard and card sets available for purchase that can be used for independent activities. William Van Cleave and Kendore Learning (https://kendorelearning.com/store/classroom-sets-c-6/) are two places that you can purchase premade morphology games and card sets.

You can make your own cards using a flashcard-making website, *AI* or *Canva* (https://www.canva.com/magic-design/) and other online programs. I often use Sightwords (https://sightwords.com/sight-words/games/) because you can make the vowels red.

If you generate your own cards, you can focus on the bases, affixes, and Greek combining forms on which you are working. You can also create decks that are customized to the work you are doing in class.

Flashcards decks are perfect for scaffolding activities without students knowing what you are doing. Students can receive different sets of cards according to their skills.

Flashcards Ideas

1. Have flashcards with bases/combining forms and their meanings. Students match the bases/combining forms with their meanings.
2. Have flashcards with affixes and meanings. Students match the affixes with the meaning cards.
3. Mix bases/combining forms and affix cards together. Students build as many words as possible. Extend this activity to spelling by having them write their words in their notebooks/binders.

The image below from The Dyslexia Classroom (https://www.thedyslexiaclassroom.com) shows handmade affix and base cards written on colored construction paper.

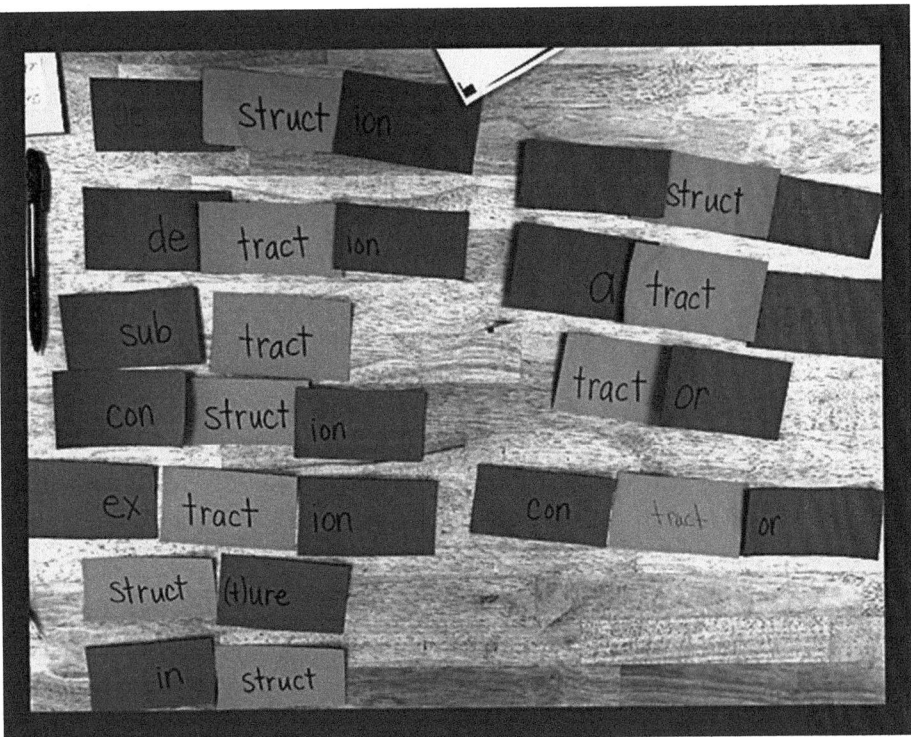

Courtesy of Casey Harrison

10. Class Lists Built Around Morphemes

If you are concerned about finding time to teach morphology, start by generating lists as a class. Each week choose a morpheme and see how many words the class can find. For example, you might start with *bio-* and students would add *biography*, *biology*, and *biodiversity*. Keep the lists either posted or in digital files so that you can add to them as students discover additional words with that morpheme. Students could also start their own class morphology book which they add to throughout the year.

11. Morpheme Word Sorts

Create word sort decks (on cards) for students to sort words by morpheme. By using decks of word cards, rather than paper/pencil sorts, the activity becomes multi-modal and much more engaging for students.

The card deck should include a range of words that contain several morphemes. The students' task is to sort the cards into morpheme groupings. You can supply the target morphemes on heading cards for sorting or have students do a blind sort where they must decide what the targeted morphemes might be.

The Word Sort Process
Part 1
1. Create groups of 2 to 4 students.
2. Students place heading cards on the desk or floor.
3. They shuffle and place word cards upside down.
4. Students take turns drawing a card, reading the word and placing it in the correct column. All players see the card and support one another in this process.

Part 2
I like to have students play a second part of the game once the cards are sorted.
1. Once the cards have been sorted into columns, students take turns giving their partner/s a clue to the meaning of one of the words in the sort. For example, if students are sorting *port* cards, Student 1 may say, "Voyageurs carried their canoe around the rapids."
2. The other student then looks at all the laid-out cards and guesses the word *portage*. If correct, students remove the *portage* card from the sort.
3. Student 2 then looks at the remaining cards and gives a clue to the meaning of a word. Students guess the new word.
4. Play continues until all the cards are back in the deck.

It can be challenging for some students to generate questions, and it may take extensive practice and modeling to build this type of flexible thinking. Part 2 will build and reinforce vocabulary for new words and words that students do not have a clear understanding of their meaning.

12. Weird Word Collections

There are many weird and wonderful words that come to us from other countries, so curating a weird word collection as a class can be engaging and worthwhile. With each new word, find and post the meaning and the country of origin (etymology) on chart paper or a bulletin board. Creating a classroom collection can be highly entertaining. Share words with the class and have them suggest words for the list. You can jumpstart this activity by posting a word each week and challenging students to find the meaning and etymology.

Mine the list for opportunities to teach vocabulary and morphology. When introducing a new word, ask students if there are word parts that indicate its meaning. What do they think the word could mean and why? Are there clues to its meaning within the word itself?

Give this activity time, as it might take a few weeks for students to fully engage, and don't be surprised when you hear your students using them throughout the day. I have listed a few examples below, but check out Gregory Venvonis' website, vowlenu.com, for other words to get you started.

Suggested Words
- *cattywampus*: something in disarray, askew
  Originating from southern United States
- *clinophile*: the love of going to bed
  Originating from clin = Latin base for lean or recline + phile = Greek base for fondness for a thing
- *dendrology*: the study of woody plants
  Originating from dendro from the Greek 'dendron' meaning trees and ology meaning the study of
- *frobly-mobly*: a way to say "not bad" when someone asks you how you are doing; cited by Charles Dickens 1870
- *gubbins*: a collection of useless items that are not so useless as to be thrown away (also called muggins)
  Originating from the United Kingdom
- *seatherny*: the serenity one feels when listening to the chirping of birds
  Originating from an English word created by using 'se' from serenity, 'ather' from feather and the suffix 'y' meaning characterized by
- *sialoquent*: tending to spray saliva while talking
  Originating from the Greek word 'sialon' meaning saliva
- *twitterpated*: infatuation/ young love
  Originating in the United States and made popular by the Disney movie "Bambi"

Stressed Syllables

Name: _____

The affix can shift the stressed vowel in a word, making the affix or base sound different. Circle the stressed syllable in each word below and note the change of pronunciation.

episode – episodic	contest – contestant
telepath – telepathy	courage – courageous
biography – biographic	captive – captivity
athlete – athletic	finite – infinity
universe – university	photograph – photography
accommodate – accommodation	recover – reply
import – important	advantage – advantageous
contribute – contribution	proverb – proverbial
music – musician	drama – dramatic
situate – situation	perfect – perfection

Exploding Bases and Greek Combining Forms

Name: _____

How many words can you find that use the following bases or Greek combining forms? Add additional words at the bottom or on the back of your paper. The first base is done for you.

bene: well	**auto:** self/same	**graph:** to write
1. Benadryl 2. benefit 3. beneficiary 4. benign 5. benediction 6. benevolent	1. 2. 3. 4. 5. 6.	1. 2. 3. 4. 5. 6.
struct: to build	**phone:** sound	**port:** to carry
1. 2. 3. 4. 5. 6.	1. 2. 3. 4. 5. 6.	1. 2. 3. 4. 5. 6.
dyna: power	**gram:** measure	**geo:** earth
1. 2. 3. 4. 5. 6.	1. 2. 3. 4. 5. 6.	1. 2. 3. 4. 5. 6.
micro: small	**trans:** across	**biblo:** book
1. 2. 3. 4. 5. 6.	1. 2. 3. 4. 5. 6.	1. 2. 3. 4. 5. 6.

Building with Affixes

Name: _____

Create 4 words for each affix.

Prefixes

un: not or opposite	**pre**: before	**re**: again
1. unhappy 2. 3. 4.	1. 2. 3. 4.	1. 2. 3. 4.
dis: not/opposite	**mis**: bad/wrong	**over**: too much
1. 2. 3. 4.	1. 2. 3. 4.	1. 2. 3. 4.

Suffixes

er: more of	**est**: most	**ful**: full of
1. 2. 3. 4.	1. 2. 3. 4.	1. 2. 3. 4.
ness: state of	**er**: person who	**less**: without
1. 2. 3. 4.	1. 2. 3. 4.	1. 2. 3. 4.

Choose 2 prefixes and 2 suffixes and write a sentence for each.

1. _____
2. _____
3. _____
4. _____

Bases and Affixes Review

Name: _____

Fill in the missing affixes and/or bases in the chart below. The first one is done for you.

	Prefix	Base	Suffix	Word
1	*dis-*	**regard**	*-ed*	**disregarded**
2	*re-*	port	*-ing*	
3		friend		unfriendly
4	*mis-*			misinformed
5		construct		reconstructed
6	*im-*		*-ing*	imprinting
7	*un-*	trust	*-ing*	
8	*semi-*			semicolons
9		vide		provider
10	*mis-*	understand	*-ing*	
11		stop		unstoppable
12		virus		antiviruses
13	*un-*	clean	*-li -ness*	
14	*mis-*			misinformed
15		health		unhealthy
16	*in-*		*-ive*	ineffective
17		circle		semicircles
18				unhealthy
19	*mid-*	year	*-s*	
20			*-ive*	unsupportive

Base and Affix Word Sort 1

Name :_____

Sort the following words into the appropriate affix box. **Write the letter** for the correct meaning of the affix at the top of each box. The first meaning is done for you.

Affix Bank:

unable	transport	happily	accomplishment
responsible	unjust	grumpiest	firmament
mistake	grandest	reportedly	transfer
misjudge	translation	rapidly	eldest
recently	unhinged	mislead	unshakeable

Meanings:

a. most   b. again   c. like/full   d. bad/wrong
e. across   f. opposite.   g. can do it   h. changes from an action to a thing

re-__b__	un- _____	trans- _____	mis- _____
reportedly recently			

-able _____	-ly _____	-est _____	-ment _____

Pembroke Publishers © 2024 *Bridging The Reading Gap* by Heather Willms ISBN 978-1-55138-367-5

Base and Affix Word Sort 2

Name : _____

Sort the following words into the appropriate affix box. **Write the letter** for the correct meaning of the affix at the top of each box. The first meaning is done for you.

Base/Form Bank:

telegraph	audition	telephone	erupt
concourse	logical	pedicure	generation
logistics	login	discourse	gentry
graphite	centipede	audience	saxophone
disrupt	rupture	gender	pediatrist
phonics	symphony	recourse	audible
photograph			

Meanings:

a. thought	b. to break	c. sound	d. foot
e. to write	f. birth/origin	g. to hear	h. run

graph __e__	log_____	pede_____	rupt_____
telegraph graphite photograph			
gen_____	aud_____	phone_____	course_____

Pembroke Publishers © 2024 *Bridging The Reading Gap* by Heather Willms ISBN 978-1-55138-367-5

Building a Matrix, Option 1

Name: _____

Example:

re-	**Teach** **-to show or explain**	-er
pre-		-able
un-		-ing

This matrix uses the word *teach*. Choose from the following words and affixes to make three of your own matrices.

Bases/Forms:

help – to aide or support   joy – happy/pleasure
hope – desire/expectation   stop – end
break – separate/interrupt   heat – warm

Affixes:

re- – again   -ing – happening now   un- – not
-able – can do it   -ed – already happened   -est – most
-ful – full of   -er – person who does it
own choice of affix

Pembroke Publishers © 2024 *Bridging The Reading Gap* by Heather Willms ISBN 978-1-55138-367-5

Building a Matrix, Option 1 (cont'd)

Create sentences using one of the bases you have chosen. Remember to use the doubling rule if needed.

Building a Matrix, Option 2 (2 pages)

Name: _____

re-		*-er*
pre-	**Teach** -to show or explain	*-able*
un-		*-ing*

This matrix uses the word *teach*. Choose from the following words and affixes and make three of your own matrices.

Bases/Forms:

struct – to build	port – to carry	
scribe – to write	ject – to throw	tract – to pull
sign – action to convey meaning	rupt – break	own choice of base/form

Affixes:

pre- – before	*dis-* – not/opposite	*con-* – with/together
re- – again	*un-* – not/opposit	*-tion* – makes a verbe
-able – can	*-ure* – act/result	*-ful* – full of
-or – person or thing who does it		own choice of affix

Pembroke Publishers © 2024 *Bridging The Reading Gap* by Heather Willms ISBN 978-1-55138-367-5

Building a Matrix, Option 2 (cont'd)

Create sentences using one of the bases you have chosen. Remember to use the doubling rule if needed.

Using Matrices

Name: _____

Create new words with the free bases below:

		ed ing s	
un	**help** *do what is needed*	er	s
		ful	ly ness
		less	ly

		ed ing s	
re un	**thank** *thought, gratitude; think, feel*	er	s
		ful less	ly ness

help: _____

_____

_____

thank: _____

_____

_____

Using Matrices (cont'd)

Name: _____

Create new words with the bound bases below:

bank

	rupt	ed
ab	*to*	ible
cor	*break*	ing
dis		ion
inter		ly
		s

a		ability
in		able
per	**spect**	ed
pro	*look at*	ing
		ion
		ive
		or
		s
dis	re	ate	or
		ful	ly
			ness

re	con		s
de			ed
			ing
in	de		ion
			or
	struct	ive	ly
	build		ity
			ness
in		ure	es
ob			ed
sub			ing
super		al	ly
infra			ism
			ist

rupt: _____

spect: _____

struct: _____

Extending: Design your own word matric by using the matrix generator:
http://www.neilramsden.co.uk/spelling/matrix/run.html?version=temp

4

Spelling

> "We can make sense of orthography by assuming that almost all letters in a printed word have a functional relationship to sound and/or meaning."
> (Moats, 2020, p. 106)

I remember doing spelling assessment three times a year with my Grade 5 students. Edmonton Spelling was an assessment where students spelled 100 words three times per year to place them on a graded continuum. Not understanding the value of the tool, I gave the screen, counted the number of words each student in my class got correct, and then compared their scores to a norms list that showed a grade-level equivalent for each score. Unfortunately, the tool did not break down the words by concept, a structure that allows the teacher to identify patterns of errors. The assessment revealed nothing to pinpoint or guide further instruction for my students.

A well-developed spelling tool is one of the easiest places to start with explicit instruction as everyone can be assessed at the same time. It can provide a snapshot of which concepts are in place, who needs small-group instruction in spelling, and where the entire class needs explicit instruction.

One of the biggest criticisms of the English language is that it is not phonetically consistent. There is an inaccurate perception that there are so many words that do not follow a pattern or rule that it is not worth the time or energy to teach phonics to students. While there are words that are not fully decodable, and therefore require special attention, over 80 percent of English words either align, or closely align, with a pattern or rule (Moats, 2005). Words that do not align are sometimes viewed as containing phonetic errors when in fact they are simply taking on a different and often more complex role.

A Teacher's Love/Hate Relationship with Spelling

I did not like teaching spelling because I knew that the programs we were using showed me *which of my students could memorize, not who could spell*. I saw no transfer to daily work, and I felt it was a waste of time. At one point I decided to remove my spelling block. I let the families of my students know that spelling work would be embedded in my daily teaching practice that year. Within two weeks of notifying parents, my administrator was at my door. Ed was a fabulous administrator, and we had a great working relationship. He opened with, "I hear you are not running a spelling program this year." When I shared why and what I hoped to do instead, I was surprised by his response. He shared that spelling was something that parents understood and knew how to help with at home. He strongly encouraged me to reinstate spelling and I did. Why? There were several reasons. I knew the importance of teaming with parents, I deeply respected my administrator, I knew I had bigger "hills to die on," and most importantly, I had no idea how to explicitly teach spelling within my regular practice.

Now that I was back to teaching spelling I needed a new plan. I had tried several programs and although there were a variety of lists that could work, none of them taught the "why" of spelling patterns. I was also so busy with all that I was required to do, I could not see myself running multiple programs and spelling lists in my room (which would meet the needs of all my students). It was just me, so I needed something that could be done as an entire class.

I came up with a two-point plan. One, I would curate my spelling lists from content words that were introduced through my curriculum. Words like *homogeneous*, *saturate*, and *solute* would come from our chemistry unit and *parallelogram*, *axis*, and *rhombus* would come from math. As an upper elementary teacher this made sense, but from a phonics perspective it was a disaster. Why? Because each list had a wide range of concepts represented in the words. The -*eous* in *homogeneous* and the silent 'h' in *rhombus* made no sense to my students and therefore they had to depend on their working memory to do well on the weekly spelling test.

My second plan (and a good one) was to curate my lists in such a way that the words that were the easiest to spell were at the beginning of the list and more complex words were at the end. This way, students who struggled with spelling were asked (in private) to do the first 5–7 words and then try the others. They would only be scored on the first 5–7 words and no one else needed to know what was in place. Students were successful with the words that had sound-to-symbol correlations, which were all frontloaded on each list. Everyone did their spelling test at the same time, which was a win for the teacher. This strategy worked so well that it is suggested for use in the lessons within this book. The difference in the lessons that follow is that everyone gets explicit instruction in phonics spelling patterns before 'working' lists of spelling words.

If Ed came to my room today, the conversation would be very different. Actually, he would not have to come to my classroom for this discussion because I am passionate about teaching spelling. As far as value for time, it is an excellent use of time if taught explicitly with pre-assessment and progress monitoring. I would probably rename it "Word Explorations" or "Word Play" to shake off the stigma of poorly taught spelling. It would include explicit phonics lessons, as well as the morphology and vocabulary lessons and activities included in this book, and it definitely would be on my schedule!

Encoding and Decoding

I have worked in many classrooms, and as a reading intervention teacher, I often worked in individual schools for multiple weeks at a time. When I start at a school, I ask teachers what they see as their greatest need. In the upper elementary grades, it is not uncommon to talk to a teacher and have them share that the reading skills in their classroom are "pretty good." My response to this comment

> Why can students read but not spell and are these two linked? In fact, they are linked. When we read, all of the letters are provided for the reader but when we spell, we must retrieve the letters in the correct order (think of orthographic-mapping, page 12).

is always, "Great, how's the spelling?" If you are teaching in these grades, you can probably guess what the response usually is. "It's terrible."

The English language has a deep orthography (it is complex). As mentioned in the introduction, there are approximately 230 letter combinations (graphemes) to spell the sounds in speech (Mather et al., 2009). Just think of ā /A/: *pain*, *pane*, *sleigh*, and *tray*.

Since decoding is looking at a string of letters on a page and matching them to the sounds that we speak and hear, encoding (spelling) can be approached the opposite way. What are the sounds that we speak or hear, and what are the matching letter/s required on the page to represent them?

One of the concerns with poor spelling in later grades is that every sound in a word is not represented on the page. I always tell students that if they have something for every sound, even if the letter combinations are not correct, I will be able to read it. It is when students are missing sounds (letters) that it is challenging to read. Using graph paper in the phoneme-grapheme activity below is a highly effective way for students to focus on the fact that every sound in a word must be represented by a grapheme (one or more letters).

An additional concern is that students do not know what spelling patterns to use and when to use them. Explicit instruction not only provides valuable information regarding how the English language is put together, but it also provides a foundation of knowledge and skills that students can turn to when they are unsure, rather than deciding if something "looks right."

An understanding of the why and the how of word construction supports students in a powerful way. I know that if I had taught or reviewed phonics and morphology with my Grade 5 classes over the years, I would have given them tools to support reading and spelling that would have taken them into high school and beyond.

Why Spelling?

There are many reasons why spelling should not be disregarded in our busy classrooms.

1. Moats (2005) states, "But all children, even those who are predisposed to be good spellers, have much to learn about the history, structure, and representation of their own language that will pay off in many other verbal domains." Explicit spelling lessons benefit all students. It is easy to understand that explicit spelling instruction is helpful for struggling readers and writers, but this work also provides foundational knowledge and linguistic understanding for our best spellers and readers. Even you, as a competent, university-trained educator, are likely to have some 'aha' moments as you work through these lessons.

2. Spelling is critical for communication in writing. If you write that you "need more time for the dessert on your holiday," because you are going to Saudi Arabia and are referring to the geographically sandy areas of the country, that is not what the reader understands. With one extra 's,' the reader thinks you hope to make time to eat a variety of sweets. Poor spelling can also be challenging for the reader if words are so misspelled that they have to labour to figure out what each word is before finding meaning in a sentence.

3. Teaching spelling expands vocabulary. Words are used to teach and practice the patterns of spelling. Educators address spelling and vocabulary when teaching the spelling patterns of English words.
4. Spelling supports reading. Spelling and reading rely on the same underlying knowledge (Moats, 2005). Knowing that a specific string of letters represents a word and meaning (orthographic mapping, page 12) is foundational for word storage and quick retrieval.
5. Spelling is about how words are put together and why. This will broaden student understanding of the English language and where it comes from (etymology). It will also provide students with knowledge to rely on when encountering an unknown word either in reading or spelling. For example, in the word cyst (which I find is consistently pronounced incorrectly), the 'c' is followed by a 'y', so explicitly taught students will know that the 'c' makes a /s/ sound because it is followed by 'y', and it is a medical term, which means it has Greek origins (it comes from the Greek word *kystis*, meaning bladder or or pouch). When applying this knowledge, students will pronounce *cyst* correctly as /sɪst/ and not /kɪst/.
6. Spelling supports fluency and comprehension. Knowledge of words, word parts, and relationships between words support access to text. The more knowledge students can apply to words and the more practice they have in reading words with specific spelling concepts, the better their fluency. Fluency allows students to focus their mental energy on comprehension rather than decoding.
7. The more students know how to spell, the more effectively they can use spell checkers and other assistive tech supports. For example, if a student wants to write the word *citizen* but they are not sure if it ends in 'sen' or 'son,' typing s-i-t-i-s-e-n into a spell checker might not help them. But, if that same student knows that /s/ can be spelled with an 's' or a 'c' (if followed by either 'e,' 'i' or 'y'), they have another option to try. The closer a student comes to the actual spelling of a word, the more likely it will be recognized by assistive tech.
8. Students who write easily tend to write more (Mather et al, 2009) and knowing how to spell makes writing a whole lot faster and easier. If students must keep stopping to consider how to spell words, valuable cognitive time and energy is taken from focusing on the flow of ideas in a written passage. Some students will only write with words that they know how to spell, which limits their ability to express their thoughts and ideas.
9. Students find spelling fascinating. Well planned and delivered lessons taught by an enthusiastic teacher are highly engaging for students. They will be asking questions, bringing words to class (especially exceptions to rules) and thinking about words in a whole new way. When I teach explicit spelling in the upper grades, I always have one or two students who get deeply engaged in the linguistics of English. It is not uncommon for me to have side conversations with these students, sharing information about linguistic degrees and careers they might want to consider because they are so interested in this work.

Where Do I Start?

How does a teacher know what spelling concepts to start with? Since teaching students is all about meeting them where they are at, the starting place for spelling is with a spelling assessment (page 167). By using a spelling assessment, you are provided with a snapshot of the spelling skills of your students. From this information you can decide which concepts can be taught to the whole class, which concepts need to be taught to a limited number of students in a small group and which concepts are in place. Without this knowledge you are taking a 'stab in the dark' (nice idiom!!) as to what instruction will be effective for your class.

A spelling assessment might show that your students need preliminary lessons before starting with the lessons in this book. These might include:

1. Review of long and short vowels
2. Review of digraphs and blends
3. The Floss Rule
4. Possessive plurals (s, es and 's)
5. The many jobs of 'y'

Check for resources from these sources: University of Florida Learning Institute (https://ufli.education.ufl.edu/foundations/toolbox/) and West Virginia Phonics at various sites.

Taking the time to review these concepts will provide the foundation students need to access the lessons in this book. UFLI, *This Is How We Teach Reading*, and West Virgina phonics will help you do foundational work.

Transfer of Concepts Studied

The goal of spelling is to have these skills transfer to daily written work and that has been a problem with spelling in the past! I found it discouraging to spend time on spelling activities and tests when there was very little transfer to daily work. Poor spelling instruction and practice strategies can be the reason that there is minimal retention of spelling patterns. Stone (2018) in her article "Activities for Practising Spelling" states that spelling activities can range from helpful to toxic so it is important to stick with helpful strategies included in the following lessons.

One way to support transfer is to incorporate context. Since correct spellings are stored in the brain more effectively when learned and used in context, include phrases along with spelling word dictation. Rather than having students only spell the word, have them write a short phrase when practising patterns and administering the spelling test. If students are spelling a word in a short phrase, they are less inclined to focus just on the word they are working with.

The words of the phrase should be easy to write and require little thinking so that cognitive energy is directed to the word being spelled. The concept is that students are in the process of writing when they reach the target word, just as they would be in authentic writing experiences. Teachers have shared that they have seen significant growth in transfer to student work when this strategy is used. You will see sample phrases in several of the spelling lists provided.

Examples of spelling phrases for dictation:

a new **vitamin**   an **independent** boy   **omit** the last one

Lesson Word Lists

The original draft of this book included curated spelling lists. In having teachers field-test these lessons, it quickly became evident that set lists are challenging because the spelling skills and needs in every classroom are different. The revised lessons now include lists of words that you can draw on to create customized lists that meet the needs of your students.

Word Lists in Bridging the Reading Gap *are organized in the following ways:*

Sound-to-symbol Lists: Every lesson has sound-to-symbol lists for **emergent readers and spellers.**

- All words in this list follow a sound to symbol (phoneme-to-grapheme) pattern and can be spelled by identifying the sounds in the word and using one letter to spell each sound (except for digraphs and the concept being taught).
- This list will include digraphs (two letters for one sound such as 'th,' 'sh,' and 'ch'). When it comes to concepts where there is more than one letter per sound (e.g., vowel teams or complex consonants), those specific concepts are included if that is the target concept of the lesson but all other sounds are represented by a letter or digraph.
- There may be multisyllable words on this list, but students should feel confident because they will be able to identify the sounds and write the letter/s for each sound. For example, 'pilgrim' has two syllables but each sound in the word is represented by one letter.

Simple/Complex Concepts: After sound-to-symbol words, the remaining words might be divided between simple and complex concepts.

- Explicit phonics instruction should teach spelling patterns starting at the simplest pattern and moving to the more complex. This works well in the lower grades, but for upper elementary/middle school students, many students have some knowledge of spelling patterns and there is a wide range of knowledge and skills within a class.
- **Simple lists** are composed of words that have simple patterns such as the floss rule (doubled f, l, s, and z at the end of a one syllable word), vowel-consonant-e and silent letters. These concepts will be explicitly taught but many students have already picked up these spelling patterns even though they do not understand the reason they are used. Your spelling assessment will flag any simple patterns that students still struggle with. These may need to be explicitly taught.
- **Complex lists** include concepts such as vowel teams, vowel 'r' and complex consonants. Remember that from a spelling perspective, it is about spelling patterns and not whether the students is being exposed to new vocabulary. Sometimes these lists are quite short and can be filled out by using words from the simple list.

Tier 1, 2, and 3 words: Some lessons include tiered lists composed of words loosely sorted into the three tiers of vocabulary (see pages 116 and 123 as examples).

- If you find yourself questioning the placement of words with Tiers 1 and 2, remember that regional dialects and exposure play a role here. What is a Tier 1 word in Vancouver might be a Tier 2 word in Halifax.
- Teachers have shared that they want spelling to be about exposure to, and the study of, new vocabulary. If you choose to work from tiered lists, it is critical that you understand that these lists contain any and all spelling patterns, which means **they contain concepts that some students may not have been taught.** This becomes a slippery slope toward memorization, rather than spelling, so be sure to make an informed decision when teaching from these lists.
- These lists are helpful when it comes to vocabulary. While this is not how I would arrange spelling lists, they are included at the request of elementary/middle school teachers and to show what they might look like.
- These lists are for advanced spellers who need the challenge and may understand the reason for spelling patterns used in English.

Creating Spelling Lists for Your Class

Spelling lists and spelling tests are **one** way to monitor student achievement and how effective instruction has been. There are many ways to go about creating lists for spelling. I often did not have support staff in my classroom and therefore did not want to run several spelling lists at one time. As mentioned above, I created a list with sound-to-symbol words at the beginning of the list and then completed the list with what I believed to be grade level words I felt were important for my students to know how to spell. I always included 1–2 challenge or bonus words to stretch my students who were strong spellers. Considering the range of spelling skills in today's classrooms, I would probably run two lists, one for emergent spellers with simple concept words that I know students have had exposure to and one with simple and complex patterns.

Possible list combinations:
- 5 emergent words and 8–10 simple words
- 5 emergent words, 5 simple and 5 complex words
- A mix of simple and complex words

Using Spelling Tests to Monitor Progress

Many teachers choose to use spelling tests to check for understanding and application. Pre- and post-tests can be insightful for you and your students. Even if students do not do well on the post-test, they should see growth. If there is little to no growth, then it is time to take another look at instruction and make some adjustments.

When using these tests, the following tips might be helpful.

1. Wednesday/Wednesday versus Monday/Friday: A lot of students miss school on Mondays and Fridays. For this reason, I ran spelling from Wednesday to Wednesday when the greatest number of students were in attendance. This took some shifting on the part of parents and students but avoided zero data for students who consistently missed the beginning and/or end of the week.

2. The pre-test, which is the same list of words used for the post-test, is administered before the lesson is taught. The lesson is then taught, students engage in activities and practice the words, and then the post-test is administered.
3. Some teachers include review weeks every 5–8 lessons to ensure that concepts have been learned and remembered. Although review lessons are helpful, it is most effective to embed review in your daily instructional practice.

You can work through the lessons in this chapter **without running spelling lists and tests**. Simply teach the concepts, engage in activities, and monitor student achievement in the "You Do" part of the lesson. Ensure that you include phoneme-grapheme work with each concept and **practice dictation** (verbally stating phrases and having students write what you say) using words that include the spelling pattern that is the lesson's focus. After a set period of explicit instruction, re-administer your chosen spelling assessment to see if instruction has been effective. If not, provide further practice of concepts where students continue to struggle.

Multiple Ways to Mark Spelling

Marking Spelling

While it might seem odd to have a "Marking Spelling" section—something is spelled correctly or it is not—there are other ways to mark spelling.

The goal of teaching spelling is that students rely on knowledge (new and old) to spell. The more they know, the more strategies and skills they have at their disposal. "Invented spelling" should be viewed as temporary as it is a result of students applying the knowledge they have about how words are put together at that point in time. As they learn more about word patterns, etymology, and word meanings, their spelling will improve so it is important to celebrate every step of their journey.

Marking Strategy 1
Marks are given for how many letters in a row are correct. This takes a bit of time and practice to mark but if your students score their spelling this way, they will be taking a very close look at the correct spelling of each word. This is cognitive monitoring behaviour and it builds independence.

For example, if the word is 'citizen' and the student spells it 'citisn'. The first 4 letters are correct so even though the word is spelled incorrectly, the student gets credit for having the first 4 letters correct. Further examples might include:

akshun (action): no correct letters = 0 pts   judj (judge): 3 pts
sindr (cinder): 3 pts   match: 5 pts

Marking Strategy 2
Students are assigned a point value based on how close to correct their spelling is:

4 pts: spelled correctly
3 pts: all sounds are represented and targeted concept has been used
2 pts: targeted concept has been used
1 pt: attempts made

The bottom line is that we are looking for growth. If students score points for what they are achieving, even if the word is not spelled correctly, they are less likely to get discouraged and will be more willing to continue to engage in lessons and activities.

Spelling Lesson Format

As previously outlined, all lessons, including the lessons in this section, follow the explicit instruction model (Archer & Hughes, 2011) of I Do/We Do/You Do.

I Do: The teacher introduces and models the concept.
We Do: The teacher and students engage in activities with the concept.
You Do: Once the teacher sees that there is understanding, students practice the concept independently.

The I Do/We Do/You Do model is not necessarily linear. You may introduce a concept and then practice the concept with your students only to realize that additional teaching and modeling is needed (I Do). In another instance students may be working on independent activities and you realize that additional instruction is required. You would return to We Do until students understand the concept.

This method of instruction allows the teacher to monitor progress and understanding and then adjust instruction as needed, a hallmark of Structured Language and Literacy.

Activities

One of the challenges of teaching phonics and word play at the upper elementary/middle school level is that activities need to meet the developmental needs of the students. If activities are seen as too young, students will be less inclined to engage. If they do not see them as meaningful, they will also be reluctant. While teachers make a significant difference in engagement by presenting material in a positive way, students are wary of material that they feel is "babyish."

The following activities have all been used with students in Grades 4–8 with positive results.

1. Phoneme-Grapheme Spelling

Using boxes or graph paper is a highly effective way for students to focus on the fact that every sound in a word must be represented by a grapheme (one or more letters).

Often, when I have taught phoneme-grapheme spelling, it is the first time some students have realized that spelling is representing the sounds in a word using letters. This is an example of why explicit instruction is so important!

When teaching this process, spend time walking through the steps as a class so students have the opportunity become comfortable with the process and consider spelling with this perspective. Many of the lessons in this chapter have included phoneme-grapheme spelling when introducing a concept. Struggling students, and those who are hesitant to make a mistake, like this activity because they know that they can copy or check what the teacher has modeled on the board, providing an opportunity for every student to succeed.

Materials

Provide graph paper for students to engage in this activity. Students with fine motor challenges may prefer larger graph paper, so it is good to provide students with a choice of paper. Graph paper can be laminated or put in plastic sleeves for reuse, although many upper elementary students view this as something that would be used for younger students.

Students can either write on every line of the graph paper or skip lines so that descending letters (e.g., p, q, g) don't interfere with the word below.

Phoneme to Grapheme Process

1. Say the word and students repeat it. For example, say *wrist*, and students say *wrist*.
2. Together the teacher and students count the sounds in the word. Students who like to physically engage in a lesson or struggle with identifying the correct number of sounds can either tap the sounds on the table, moving from left to right (the way text is read), or counting with their fingers. As teachers, we are sometimes concerned that students will not want to physically count the sounds, but I often see adults using their fingers when engaging in this activity in a workshop.
3. When the class agrees that there are four sounds or phonemes in *wrist*, they put a dot at the bottom of the correct number of graph boxes to correlate with the correct number of sounds. They can also use a line. Students who are good at spelling may say there are five sounds because they can visualize the word and know there are five letters. This is a great opportunity to review the concept that more than one letter can be used to represent one sound. In the case of *wrist*, the 'wr' represent the sound /r/.

_	_	_	_	

4. Together, write the letters in the marked boxes. Once the word is written in the graph, model it on the board. Students check that their word is correct.
5. Have students write a short phrase at the end of the graph. For example, "a bent wrist" or "he bent his wrist."

wr	i	s	t	a bent wrist
_	_	_	_	

6. Some students will not need to mark the boxes with dots/lines and can move directly to writing the letters in the graph boxes. The dots/lines act as a scaffold for those who need them.

Not all words are suitable for this activity. Words with schwa and highly unusual spellings defeat the purpose of this activity. For example, the word *one* would not be good to graph because the first sound does not have a letter to represent it, then there is a schwa, the 'n' (which is easy to graph) and a silent 'e.'

Samples of student work:

2. Spelling Dictation

Spelling dictation that includes target words within a phrase or sentence is a powerful spelling activity as it provides context. Using sentence dictation allows for embedded instruction and review of grammar such as capitals and periods, as well as modeling how sentences are put together to create meaning (semantics). Dictation also provides the opportunity to spell the target word while engaging in writing which makes for an authentic spelling experience and supports transfer of proper spelling to daily written work.

Use any of the words from the lesson word lists to practice dictation in spelling lessons. You can make dictation into a game by providing points for punctuation, grammar, and the correct spelling of the target word.

3. Spelling Concepts in Print

While this was addressed in Chapter 2: Vocabulary, reading spelling words in print also supports spelling. This includes both reading word lists and reading target words in connected text.

When reading words in connected text, ensure that the text is not too difficult for the reader. The goal is to recognize and practice reading spelling concepts in print, not to spend a significant amount of time on decoding and comprehension.

Word lists included with each spelling lesson are also a great source for word reading activities. Simply post or project a list and practice reading it until the class is fluent and able to read it at a speaking pace. Students can also do this work independently or in small groups, and lists can be sent home for additional reading practice once the concepts have been taught and practiced at school.

Students who read well have strong Rapid Automatic Naming (RAN), but struggling readers do not. While the jury is out on whether this can be taught, reading word lists is a concise way to reinforce a spelling pattern.

4. Word/Speed Drawing

As mentioned in Chapter 2: Vocabulary, drawing words may seem like a soft skill activity but if a student does not understand a word and its use, they will not be able to generate a drawing. While this chapter focuses on spelling, students will be encountering new words through the word lists, and it is important that they understand what they are spelling (orthographic mapping). You will see word drawing as an activity throughout the spelling lessons, with students writing the **target words** in each box before the game begins.

5. Synonym/Antonym Challenge

Choose one or more spelling words and come up with three (or more) words with a similar or opposite meaning.

For example:
goblet: glass, cup, chalice, wine glass, tumbler, stemware
arrive: depart, leave, exit, go, vamoose

Having students do this work in pairs or small groups provides an opportunity for oral language development. Students will be talking about words and will have to decide which of the group's suggestions are the best words to use.

6. Wordle

The New York Times (NYT) game Wordle took the world by storm in 2022, and it is still played with enthusiasm today. You can simply project the NYT daily Wordle (https://www.nytimes.com/games/wordle/index.html) onto your board each day or use NYT Wordle for Kids (https://wordle-nyt.org/wordle-for-kids).

Make the most of this game by discussing phonics concepts as you work together to solve the puzzle. Include questions like:

See page 168 for links to other word games.

- "Could it be a vowel team?"
- "What vowel teams use 'o' (or 'a,' 'e,' 'u,' or 'i')?"
- "Is it a diagraph?"
- "Why can't you use 'j' at the end?"

7. You're the Editor

Editing is a great way to incorporate connected text into spelling. This activity can be done several times a week with minimal use of time. On paper, it works well as a start-of-day activity because students can come into class and work on the edits before class begins.

- Choose or create (with AI) a written paragraph that includes multiple words using the week's target concept. You can also review previous concepts taught by including them in the edit paragraph.
- Edit the paragraph so that it contains 5-6 errors. Errors can be with spelling and/or punctuation.
- Project the paragraph on the board and have students correct the inaccuracies together. The paragraph can also be written, and students find and correct spelling errors independently or in pairs.
- If using paper, review corrections all together.

There are books and websites that have ready-made passages to correct. One of the most popular ones is Daily Edits on Education World: https://www.educationworld.com. This site has numerous passages organized by month and it's free!

8. 50/50

Ann Richmond Fisher has created an amazing number of great spelling games that can be found on spelling-words-well.com. Ann is also the creator of www.word-game-world.com.

50/50, one of Ann's games, is about manipulating words to create new words. You can **scaffold this activity** by having different target word cards and instructions based on the roll of the dice.

Players: 2
Skill: Spelling, word play, vocabulary
Grade level: 4-8
Supplies: Word cards, one standard die, answer key, paper and pencil to keep score

Preparation
1. Print out Ann's word cards and laminate them if possible. You can also make your own word cards. (Ann's site has cards that contain words from her 4/5 grade lists. It's best to choose words that aren't too long.)
2. Cut the cards and print the guidelines to keep at your desk as a reference.
3. Create a poster of these guidelines and place near the cards:
    - If a 1 or 2 is rolled, add one letter to the word and earn 2 points.
    - If a 3 or 4 is rolled, subtract a letter from the word and earn 4 points.
    - If a 5 is rolled, change one letter to make another word and earn 5 points.
    - If a 6 is rolled, rearrange all the letters in the word and earn 6 points.

To Play
1. Shuffle the cards and place them face down on the table.
2. Player 1 turns over a card and rolls the die.
3. They try to form a new word, following the game guidelines. To earn points, the player must also use the new word correctly in a sentence.
4. Each time a player forms a new word, they may rearrange the letters in the original word. Note: It is not always possible to form a new word.

6. Player 2 takes their turn in the same manner.
7. If a player is unable to form a new word following the guidelines above, they do not receive points for that turn, and the other player takes their turn.
8. If a player draws LOSE A TURN, they cannot make a new word on that turn.
9. If a player draws TAKE AN EXTRA TURN, they draw a word card, roll a die, and can earn points. They repeat the process with the extra turn card.
10. Play continues until someone scores 50 points. The first player to 50 points wins.

Examples:

Player 1 draws the word *quiet* and rolls a 3. They subtract 'e' and spell *quit*. They receive 4 points.

Player 2 draws the word *couch* and rolls a 1. They add 'r' and spell *crouch*. They receive 2 points.

9. Word Seekers

This is a great review activity.

1. Create word cards using words with the spelling concepts you have taught. Create 6-8 decks of cards so that each team has the same set of word cards. You can scaffold this activity by making a deck or two that uses the spelling patterns you have taught, but the words are all emergent, sound to symbol spellings. These decks would be handed to emergent spellers.
2. Divide students into teams.
3. Students open their set of cards and place the words face up on the table.
4. Call out a spelling concept and students find a word or words that use that rule. For example, the teacher asks students to find a word that uses hard 'c'. Students look at their cards and find the word *coach*. They hold it up for you to check.
5. This game works exceptionally well for reviewing vowel teams. You can either ask for a specific team like 'oa' or you can ask for a word that has a vowel team that makes a specific sound, for example the long 'O' sound.

10. Is it Spelled Correctly?

This game is also great for review.

1. Students have a sheet of lined paper that has been folded lengthwise (hotdog fold). This creates two vertical columns on the page.
2. At the top of one column students write Correct and at the top of the second column, they write Incorrect.
3. Write a target word on the board and either spell it correctly using the current spelling pattern being taught, or incorrectly using a spelling that is close to the correct spelling. For example, if the lesson is on 'tch,' write huch or luntch.
4. Use the word in a sentence.
5. Students write the word in the appropriate column. If you use the word luntch, they would write it in the incorrect column.

6. After each word, discuss the rationale for where the word should be placed. Students who have placed the word incorrectly move the word to the correct column before proceeding with the game.
7. Students can take turns leading this game either as a class or in small skill-level groups. The process of creating correctly or incorrectly spelled words and generating sentences reinforces knowledge of correct spellings.

11. It's Up to You!

This game is like "Is It Spelled Correctly?" but it includes both correctly and incorrectly spelled words.

1. Write two spellings of the same word on the board, one correct and one incorrect (e.g., judge and judj).
2. Have students write the correct spelling in their notebooks/binders.
3. Erase the incorrect answer. Students check to see if they have the word written correctly.

Extension activity: Divide the class into two groups and have a contest to see how many each team gets correct. Allow team discussions.

12. Word Families

This is a great game to play with the class, in pairs, or as an independent activity. It works well when you have small amounts of time to fill or as a warmup for other word work.

1. Choose a word that contains the concept you are targeting in your lesson. For example, if you are working on the complex consonant 'dge' you might choose the word *judge*.
2. Students write as many words with judge as they can. Their list might include *judges, judged, judging, rejudge, judgeable, judgement, rejudges, misjudge*, and *prejudge*.

Through this activity students will be spelling the target concept repeatedly, thinking about word meaning and working with affixes. Win, Win, Win!

13. Spelling BINGO

At the beginning of a new concept, pass out Bingo cards. Through the week ask students to pick their choice of activities to create the BINGO of your choice (e.g., line, X, blackout). Bingo cards can be all the same or you can shuffle the concepts on each card. Laminate to prolong the life of the cards.

Card Activity Guidelines:

- Target words are words that contain the concept you are currently teaching – See word lists.
- Word Connections.
- Crossword puzzles and word searches: Allow students to use an online generator.

- Sentence and paragraph writing: They have to make sense!
- Word hunt: Dictionaries and word lists do not count.
- Word families: See activity instructions above.

Make a crossword puzzle using 12 target words.	Create a daily edit using 5-6 target words. See if a classmate can find and correct all of the errors.	Create a Word Connection game using 5-6 target words.	Using 6 target words, create a poem or rap. Perform it for someone.
Using 5 target words, find out the language of origin for each one (e.g., Latin, Greek, Anglo-Saxon).	FREE	Write one sentence using as many of the target words as you can. Continue making sentences until you have used all the words.	Choose 6 target words and add affixes to them. How many new words can you create just by adding prefixes and suffixes?
Write a paragraph including 6 target words.	Draw a cartoon strip and use 5 target words in the speech bubbles.	Write the definitions of 5 target words.	Create word families for 5 target words.
Choose 5 target words and write 3 synonyms for each.	Word Hunt: Find 6 target words in the classroom. Write down where they can be found.	Choose 5 target words and write 3 antonyms for each.	Create a word search that includes 12 target words.

14. Create a Class Dictionary of Canadian and American Spellings

Why are there differences between Canadian and American spellings? The short answer is that Canada is one of several Commonwealth countries and as such inherited British spellings, many of which remain in place today.

A Brief History Lesson

In 1755, Englishman Samuel Johnson published his 40,000-word *Dictionary of the English Language*. Before Johnson's dictionary, English spellings were not standardized (Ethier, 2017). Johnson didn't try to reform spelling to make it more logical. Instead, he simply chose the most common spellings in use at the time. Canada follows Johnson's standardized spellings with some exceptions. One notable exception is that Johnson ended 'ic' words with 'ick' (e.g., magick, musick, and comick).

In 1828, American Noah Webster published the *American Dictionary of English Language*. As an indication that the United States was no longer ruled by Britian, attempts were made to make English spellings more logical (Spellingzone.

com). Webster's 1828 dictionary and 1829 speller became the primary spelling references for generations of Americans.

Over time, American spellings began to seep across the border. Sir John A. Macdonald felt strongly that Canadian spellings should align with English spellings. He decided that all government documents should align with British practices, and this helped to retain British spellings in Canada.

Canada has made some shifts to American spellings. While we adhere to many British spellings, we have also rejected some British spellings, such as *tyre*, *kerb*, and *aluminium*. Most computer spell checking systems are American so they highlight Canadian spellings as inaccurate and will suggest changing them to American spellings.

Discuss with the students how, in the example of Samuel Johnson's 1755 dictionary, Johnson captured words in the way they were spelled at the time. Languages shift over time as new words and new spellings are incorporated into a country's general lexicon.

Ask students to create a class list of Canadian vs American spellings that they see in the media, in learning resources, and in their work. Some will be familiar (colour vs color, analyse vs analyze) and others less so (spelt vs spelled).

For a comprehensive list of words students may consider, share Improving Your English (https://improving-your-english.com/british-american-english/spelling/). This list comprises British spellings that have informed some of our Canadian spellings. Students can create a class dictionary of words that they spell following either Canadian or American patterns.

Lessons

Lesson 1: Open and Closed Syllables

Description of Concepts

Closed Syllable: When a syllable or single-syllable word consists of a vowel, followed by one or more consonants, the vowel sound is short (cat, slip, crush). The final consonant(s) "close" the vowel, so it is called a closed syllable.

Open Syllable: When a syllable or single-syllable word ends in a vowel, the vowel sound is long (me, go, she). There is no final consonant(s) to close the vowel, so it is called an open syllable.

Open and closed syllables are two of the Six Syllable Rules that guide the breaking of multisyllable words into individual syllables and determine whether the vowel sound is short or long.

Materials List: 5 ½' x 8 ½' card stock or tag board for houses, graph paper for spelling, 8 ½" x 11" copy paper for speed drawing, document camera

I Do **Start with syllable review:**
- Review how to find syllables in words. Have students hum words to determine how many syllables make up the word. Words you could use for this activity include *goblet* (2) *apple* (2) *vet* (1) *paper* (2) *banana* (3) *syllable* (3) *erupt* (2) *camera* (3) *house* (1).
- Remind students that in writing every syllable must have a vowel.
- Explain to students that when a syllable or single-syllable word consists of a vowel, followed by one or more consonants, the vowel sound is short (cat, slip, crush). The consonant "closes" the vowel, so it is called a **closed** syllable. When a syllable or single-syllable word ends in a vowel, the vowel sound is long (me, go, she). There is no consonant to "close" the vowel, so it is called an **open** syllable.

We Do **Choose from the activities below**
Phonological Awareness:
- Tell students that you are going to read a list of open and closed syllable words (see word lists below) and ask students to say "open" or "closed" to indicate whether the word is made up of an open or closed syllable. For example: *he* (open), *cut* (closed), *crunch* (closed). Students don't see the word.
- When students become skilled at identifying open and closed syllables, introduce words with two syllables and have them identify whether they are Open-Open, Closed-Closed, Closed-Open, Open-Closed (see word lists below). You can even include three-syllable words for students who are proficient with two-syllable words. This activity should be enjoyable for students, even though they will be hard at work thinking and listening.

Word Reading

Word reading supports decoding and storage of multisyllable words.
- With a document camera, project the **Activity Word List** (page 112) on the board and ask students to read them aloud together. Check that they are reading the open syllable words with a long vowel sound.

110   Chapter 4: Spelling

- Using the same list, ask students to read the list aloud together again and read only the closed syllable words.
- Repeat (with the same list) but ask students to read only the open syllable words. You can have a student come up and point to words as the class reads.

Open and Closed Syllable Houses

If appropriate for your class, create Open and Closed syllable houses to provide students with a visual of the concept. These are excellent if you use interactive notebooks in your class.

Instructions:

1. Place a 5 1/2" × 8 1/2" piece of card stock on each desktop in the landscape position.
2. Fold over one third of the card to create the door. For students with fine motor skill concerns, score their card so that there is a predetermined line for them to fold.
3. Create the top of the roof by cutting a triangle on each side of the top third of the card. Students may find it helpful to mark the roof with a pencil before cutting.
4. Write a chosen word on the card with the open syllable on the large section of card and the last letter (to close the syllable) on the door flap.
5. Add windows and decorative touches.

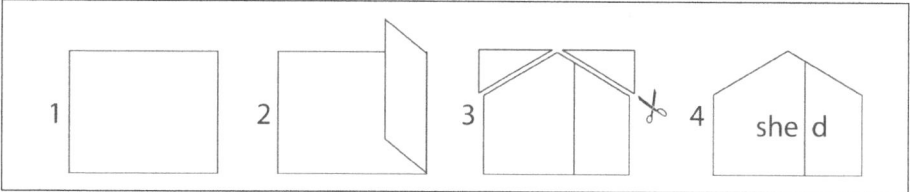

6. Once the house is constructed, students write as many open and closed words as they can on the back of their house. Students can look at other students' houses to get ideas for additional words.

    For example: *no/not, go/got, she/shed, he/help, hi/him, we/wet.*

You Do Choose from the activities below:

Speed Drawing:

Reading/spelling is all about meaning so teach or review the meaning of the words that are chosen before doing this activity. Instructions for Speed Drawing can be found on page 37.

Lessons 111

Choose 8 of the following words:
Protract – to lengthen or extend
Goblet – a drinking glass with a stem
Hobo – short for "homeward bound" – coined during the Great Depression
Erupt – eject lava, ash, or gases
Omit – to leave out or exclude
Torso – trunk of the body
Erode – to gradually wear away
Cargo – goods carried on a ship, plane, or vehicle
Veto – the right to reject a decision or proposal
Gigantic – huge, very big (Gigantic starts with a soft 'g'. If you have not taught this lesson, do not choose this word.)

Identifying Open/Closed Syllables
Using words from the word list below, have students write them in their notebook/binder and identify if they are Open-Open, Open-Closed, Closed-Closed, and so on.

frozen – OC	hobo – OO	instruct – CC
erupt – OC	zero – OO	construct – CC
goblet – CC	silent – OC	ransack – CC
omit – OC	catnap – CC	protract – OC

Synonym Challenge
Using words from the lists below, have students write a word and then think of three words with a similar meaning (synonyms). Challenge students to find as many synonyms as possible. Extend this activity by finding antonyms.
For example: goblet: glass, cup, chalice, wine glass, tumbler, stemware

Spelling Tests:
Spelling tests are not included for this lesson as it is a concept-based lesson rather than a pattern-based lesson.

    Instead, engage students in dictation. Have students write a short sentence or phrase rather than just the word. Examples from the word list might include:

a small **marigold**	a new **vitamin**	he is from **Mexico**
an **independent** boy	a firm **reprimand**	an old **performer**
protract the leg	a glass **goblet**	**omit** the last one

Phonemic Awareness Activity Word List

stamp	he	start	my	end
gob	mitt	tri	go	tract
re	ramp	non	struct	grand
rupt	hi	fro	first	

Word Reading Activity to Project

stamp	he	start	my	gob
mitt	tri	tract	re	ramp
struct	non	mow	par	ne
rupt	hi	fro	first	end
po	ma	tri		

Word List

Open Syllable Words	Closed Syllable Words
be, dry, go, he, hi, I, me, no, ply, she, sly, so, try, we, why	brand, cast, cat, chin, chip, crumb, fin, fish, flat, fun, glad, got, grin, lamb, not, now, pen, pot, shack, shin, slim, slap, slip, stamp, thin
Open-Open Syllables	**Open-Closed Syllables**
ago, baby, ego, halo, hero, hobo, judo, oboe, photo, polo, silo, solo, veto, tidy, yoyo, zero	bacon, bisect, bonus, defense, edict, erode, erupt, even, frozen, hotel, human, music, open, over, prolong, protect, protract, reject, relax, result, robot, unit, vital
Closed-Closed Syllables	**Closed-Open Syllables**
admit, atom, bandit, cactus, cartoon, catnap, construct, contest, enchant, goblet, hardship, helmet, inflict, instruct, invest, laptop, lesson, metal, misfit, mitten, pencil, pumpkin, punish, ransack, solid	also, cargo, echo, gumbo, happy, hello, messy, money, presto, puppy, tango, tempo, torso, yellow
Closed-Open-Closed Syllables	**Open-Open-Closed Syllables**
acrobat, computer, dinosaur, jellyfish, marigold, principal, reprimand, stimulus	ladybug, photograph, violin
Open-Closed-Open Syllables	**Open-Open-Open Syllables**
piano	potato, radio, tomato
Closed-Closed-Closed Syllables	**Closed-Open-Open Syllables**
animal, basketball, fantastic, pajamas, president, principal, vanishing, venison	barbeque, broccoli, video, volcano
Open-Closed-Closed Syllables	**Closed-Closed-Open Syllables**
gigantic, recommend, vitamin	balcony, buffalo, camera, elephant, family, gravity, multiply, performer, spaghetti, tendency

Lesson 2: Schwa

Schwa (ə) is the most common vowel sound in the English language, but many educators find schwa challenging to teach. It shows up in many words and it makes decoding and spelling difficult. This means that understanding and being able to identify schwa will strengthen reading and spelling skills.

Hopefully this important concept has been introduced and/or taught early to your students, as high-frequency tricky words contain schwa (e.g., the, of, come). If not, this will be a valuable lesson for all students.

The Sound of Shwa

Without getting technical, schwa is a relaxed sound that can replace any of the vowels (a, e, i, o, u). The sound of schwa is similar to the /u/ sound in 'butter' but it can change slightly depending on where it is in the word and what letters are on either side of the vowel. Sometimes schwa can be referred to as a lazy "u" which, although is not technically correct, can be helpful to students. Sometimes schwa can be a short, soft 'i' sound (e.g., salad). It is softer and weaker than short /ŭ/ or /ĭ/.

Schwa can also be present without having a letter attached to it, as in consonant-le words like apple. In consonant-le words, the schwa is voiced between the consonant and the 'l,' while the 'e' is silent (e.g., maple, turtle, able).

The Schwa Symbol

The symbol for schwa is an upside down 'e' (ə) which can be placed over the vowel that makes the schwa sound.

$$\text{th}\underset{\_}{e} \qquad \text{princip}\underset{\_}{a}\text{l} \qquad \underset{\_}{a}\text{ssume}$$

Where Can Schwa Be Found?

Schwa is found in unstressed words and in the unstressed syllables of multisyllable words.

The presence of schwa in a word can be dependent on regional dialects. For example, in Canada we voice the /er/ sound in words ending in 'er' whereas in Australia, the 'er' is often a schwa. In Canada we say /butter/ whereas in areas of Australia it is pronounced /buttu/. We have many regional dialects in Canada, but Newfoundland is probably the most distinct. Students who speak in the beautiful and unique Newfoundland dialect have to switch code when writing in standard English because their pronunciation is quite different than those represented in standard spellings.

Teaching Schwa

When teaching schwa, I tell students that the vowel acts as a double agent: it is written as one sound but says another.

It might be helpful to explain to students that the schwa sound can replace any of the vowels, rather than saying that any vowel can represent the schwa sound. This is a small shift but may be helpful, especially when it comes to spelling.

The Rule

I Do

- Take a few minutes to discuss a double agent. Students will love this conversation and it will help them to understand the behaviour of schwa vowels. Double agents appear to work for one country or agency but are, in fact, secretly working for another. After discussing double agents, share that in today's lesson you will be talking about vowels that act like a double agent: they look like they should say one thing, when in fact they say something else entirely.

- Depending on the age and skill level of your students, explain that English is a stress-timed language. That means that the most important words in a sentence or message are stressed. These are usually nouns, verbs, adjectives, and adverbs.

- Have students say, "I went to the mall." Ask them which is the stressed word in that sentence? I **went** to the mall.
- Continue with these sentences. He **hit** the ball first. He bought a new **bike**. My **iphone** is broken. Sentences can have more than one stress word like: **Let's** go the **park**. Students may have heard two stress words in the sentence, "He **bought** a new **bike**" and they would not be wrong. The important part of this lesson is to focus on sentences having stress words, not to get tangled up in what is or is not a stress word.
- Once you have looked at stress words in sentences, share with students that words also have stress syllables.
- Review syllables at this time if necessary:
  - Words can be divided into syllables.
  - Every written syllable requires a vowel.
  - You can find syllables easily by asking students to hum the word. If they hum banana, they will find it has three syllables.
- Ask students what the stressed syllable is in **wag**on, ban**an**a, **sal**ad, and um**brel**la.
- Look at each of these words again and point out that one of the vowels does not do what we expect it to do, just like a double agent.
  - Wag-on – the 'o' makes a soft, short 'u' or short 'i' sound depending on where you live.
  - Sal-ad – the second 'a' makes a soft, short 'i' sound.
  - Ba-na-na – the 'a' in ba **and** the last na make a short 'u' sound.
- These vowels make a soft, short 'u' sound, as in 'butter' or a short, soft ''i' sound as is 'kid.' These are called schwa. Schwa is the most common vowel sound in English.
- The schwa sound can be made by any vowel.
- There is a symbol for schwa, which is an upside down 'e' and looks like this: ə. Write the examples on the board.

ə   ə   ə
th<u>e</u>   princip<u>a</u>l   <u>a</u>ssume

We Do
- Project or write words containing schwa on the board (see lists below). Identify and draw a line under the stress syllable. Once this is done for all words, identify schwa in each word by placing the schwa symbol 'ə' above the appropriate vowel.
- Begin by marking the syllables and then schwa as students identify them. Once they are confident, have students come up to the board and do this work.

You Do

There are many schwa words listed below. Because this is not a specific spelling concept, use any of the vocabulary activities and teach meaning and schwa at the same time.

For example, you may choose to do speed drawing but have students identify and mark the schwa before they begin to draw.

Spelling Test

Spelling tests are not included for this lesson as it is a concept-based lesson rather than a pattern-based lesson. You may choose to do some dictation of phrases and short sentences using schwa words.

Schwa Word Lists

Tier 1 Words		Tier 2 Words		Tier 3	
about	helmet	abundant	general	algebra	medical
accident	horrible	account	generous	alkaline	medicine
alphabet	jacket	achieve	habitual	astronaut	microscope
angel	lemon	alert	human	astronomy	mineral
animal	London	analyze	income	atlas	molecule
April	memory	apparent	item	biology	orchestra
around	necessary	approach	kingdom	carnivore	organism
award	open	aroma	legal	chemical	parliament
away	other	assume	locket	chemistry	particle
bagel	parrot	attention	method	climate	rhombus
balloon	president	authority	model	curriculum	technology
banana	principal	avoid	mucus	cylinder	variable
below	problem	benefit	natural	data	
bikini	raisin	calendar	occur	decibel	
bottom	reason	capital	pasta	decimal	
broken	remember	cavity	pelican	denominator	
busy	responsible	cinema	pilot	element	
button	ribbon	commission	political	evolution	
children	rocket	common	possible	experiment	
comma	salad	community	principle	geology	
cousin	season	consequence	significant	harmony	
difficult	second	consistent	similar	hypothesis	
dinosaur	silent	counsel	specific	legislate	
doctor	sofa	define	system		
elephant	sugar	director	victim		
eleven	thousand	economy	wisdom		
enemy	ticket	effect	witness		
family	tomorrow	electric			
gorilla	umbrella	fossil			
	zebra				

Notes:
- Check the academic word list for additional Tier 2 words containing schwa.
- The word lists above do not use schwa in place of the letter 'u' as these can be difficult to determine when first learning to identify schwa. Schwa in place of the letter 'u' can also be dependent on regional dialects.

Lesson 3: Vowel-Consonant-e or Magic 'e'

Materials: graph paper

It is impossible to teach the role of vowel-consonant-e (sometimes referred to as magic 'e') without understanding open and closed syllables. When a vowel is followed by a consonant (closed syllable), it makes a short vowel sound (e.g., fin, rat, nod). In each of these examples, there are three sounds in each word and three letters — one letter for each sound. When writing the word fine, rate or node, there are still 3 sounds in each word, but the vowel sound is now long. The spelling f-i-n will not work for the word "fine" because the 'n' after the 'i' makes it short.

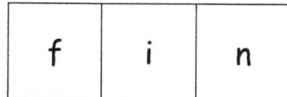

Since it is not possible to add another sound to the word, the way to make the 'i' in 'fine' long is to add a silent 'e.' Essentially the 'e' reaches back and makes the short vowel sound long. This is called a **diacritic** (a letter or letters that affect the sound of those near it). Magic 'e' is one of the many roles that silent 'e' plays in English spelling.

Phoneme-grapheme spelling is an excellent way to demonstrate this concept. When graphing magic 'e' words, the 'e' cannot have its own box because it is silent, so it is placed in the same box as the last consonant.

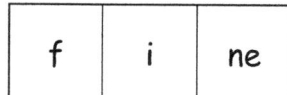

Unless there is a suffix (e.g., electives or gated) this pattern will be found at the end of words.

Why is this important for syllable work? The vowel-consonant-e pattern (magic-e) must stay together when decoding multisyllable words.. When teaching how to decode multisyllable words, a short review of 'ate,' as in 'rebate' and 'contemplate,' will help struggling readers who may not have been taught this concept in earlier grades.

I Do   Using the information above, explain the role of magic 'e.' Model words with magic 'e' on a graph to show how the silent 'e' does not make a sound but impacts the vowel before the consonant.

Check with lower grades in your school to see what language they are using for vowel-consonant-e so that you can keep the language consistent. For example, if grade 1/2 teachers are using the term 'bossy-e,' use that term rather than introducing the term 'magic-e' as this can create confusion for students.

Phoneme-Grapheme Spelling

We Do   Hand out graph paper and have students graph words that contain magic 'e.' Consider using both one syllable and multisyllable words so everyone can access the lesson at their skill level.

Read lists of words with the magic 'e' pattern. Draw from the word lists below.

You Do   Choose from the activities below:
Speed Drawing: This is a great activity for magic 'e' as there are many words that will align with vocabulary you are working with in class.
"50-50": page 105
"You're the Editor": page 105
"Spelling Bingo": page 107

Spelling Tests
This is a great place to begin spelling tests.

- Choose appropriate words from the following lists and create the desired number of lists.

- Decide whether to do a pretest **and** post-test.
- When administering the post-test, remember to have student write a short phrase with the word, rather than just the word.

Word List Vowel-Consonant-e					
Sound-to-Symbol			Simple Concepts		Complex Concepts
adore	galore	shade	accuse	fluke	chrome
amuse	glare	shame	acute	immune	concentrate
beware	grade	shape	allude	include	dilapidated
bile	grape	shave	arrive	ozone	dissipate
blade	grave	shore	assume	recede	dredge
blame	haze	sire	athlete	redemption	foresee
blare	hire	site	aware	salute	gadget
blaze	ignore	skate	before	scale	glitch
brake	impure	slate	change	scare	headache
brute	kite	slave	chute	sincere	manipulate
chase	maze	smoke	commune	stampede	microscope
chose	mime	snake	commute	stovetop	phoneme
compose	mine	snare	compare	strange	ratchet
compute	mistake	spade	compete	suppose	scheme
confuse	pave	spare	complete	therefore	sphere
costume	pile	spoke	concrete	these	tightrope
crave	plate	square	delete	whale	wretch
craze	pothole	stare	describe	whole	
crude	prone	theme	dilute		
decline	prude	tire	exclude		
defuse	prune	trade	excuse		
dispute	quake	tribute	explode		
drape	quote	vile	explore		
flare	rave	vine	expose		
flute	reptile	volume	extreme		
	reuse	waste	exude		

Lesson 4: Silent Letters kn, gn, wr, bt, gh, mb

In this lesson, silent letter pairs are referred to as digraphs; two letters that make one sound. These differ slightly from regular digraphs (e.g., 'th,' 'sh,' 'ch') in that only one letter is voiced rather than two letters that make a new sound. This makes them more challenging to spell.

Teacher Background Knowledge
This lesson may need to be broken into two lessons because words with silent letters do not follow set patterns and therefore depend on memory. This can be challenging for emergent readers and spellers.

There are two main reasons for silent letters in English:

1. Silent letters can help **differentiate homophones** (words that sound the same but have different spellings). Examples include *hour* and *our*, *knot* and *not*, or *knew* and *new*.

2. Some silent letters give insight into the origin of a word—their etymology. For example, the 'tz' in *tzar* indicates it is not of English origin but is a Russian word.

Many people think that the way English is put together does not make sense and one reason is because of what appear to be 'unnecessary' silent letters. Silent letters can be found at the beginning, middle, and end of words. If you include vowel teams, approximately 60 percent of English words contain silent letters (Dubosarsky, 2009) and almost every letter in the alphabet plays the role of a silent letter in at least one word!

To make silent letters even more tricky, some of these digraphs have a silent letter at the beginning of the pair (kn, gn, bt, wr) and with others, the silent letter is at the end of the pair (mb, gh).

All of this is to say that silent letters are tricky!

A Look at Etymology
'kn'
'Kn' is an Old English spelling with Germanic roots. Originally the 'k' would have been pronounced. The word *knight* would have been pronounced as *kniht* and "knot" as *cnotta*. Since 'kn' is awkward to pronounce, over time the 'k' was dropped but the spelling was retained. Now the 'k' is silent, so knight is pronounced the same as *night* and *knot*, the same as *not*. (Ginseng English, n.d.)

'Kn' words do have one pattern that can be helpful for spellers. 'Kn' often indicates something that is sharp (knife, knee, knit). Of course, this does not refer to all 'kn' words (e.g., know), but it can be helpful.

'gh'
'Gh' is found in Italian words like *ghetto* and *spaghetti*, and the 'h' is inserted to retain the soft /g/ sound (page 133). If students have not been taught hard and soft 'g' yet, you can simply explain that in Italian words with 'gh,' the 'h' is silent.

'mb'
'Mb' can be found in several languages of origin. Words like *climb* and *lamb* come from Old English. *Climb* was originally 'climban' and 'an' was dropped somewhere in the 1300s.

Bomb comes from the Portuguese word 'bomba,' which means the same thing; a case containing explosives.

Thumb appears to be a rogue case, because here the 'b' is not etymological but there may have been influence from the word *thimble*.

There are approximately 20 words that end in 'mb' with *bomb, climb, comb, dumb, limb, numb,* and *lamb* being the main ones.

'wr'
'Wr' is a silent letter pair where the 'w' is often used to distinguish between two words (e.g., wrap-rap, wring- ring and wrote-rote). It can be helpful for students to note that quite a few 'wr' words refer to twisting: *wrestle, wrap, wreath, wrinkle, wretch, wrench,* and *wrist*.

Other digraphs with silent letters
Other less common letter pairs are 'bt' as in *debt*, 'gn' as in *sign* and "mn" as in *column* (see Greek lesson on page 140).

Materials:
- Lined paper for activity
- Graph paper from phoneme-grapheme spelling

I Do — Using the information above, talk with students about silent letters.
- Ask students to name some silent letters found in words. Students will probably come up with vowel teams, magic-e (gate, late) and other combinations. Ask, "Why do you think we have silent letters in English? Why not leave them out?"
- Share that there are two main reasons we have silent letters in English. Hopefully this is a very interesting conversation as students puzzle out why words might have silent letters.
- Share that they can be found at the beginning, middle and end of words.
- Share that sometimes the first letter is silent and sometimes the second. Ask students for examples of both. Help them list the five main pairs that are included in this lesson.
- Talk about some of the etymological roots of pairs with silent letters.

We Do
- Write the silent letter digraphs that this lesson focuses on ('kn,' 'gn,' 'wr,' 'gh,' and 'mb') on the white board and see how many words students can think of that start with or include these letter pairs.
- Using graph paper and **phoneme-grapheme spelling**, (page 101) spell list words together. This is an important activity for silent letters, as students will see that the digraph will be placed in one box. For example, *bomb* has three sounds and requires three boxes, *b-o-mb*. Emergent spellers should be able to participate as the work is done together.

Graphic

b	o	mb	

- Play "Is it spelled correctly?" Instructions can be found on page 106. Possible word list and sentences:
    - Gost: There is a ghost costume at the Halloween store.
    - Knob: Turn the knob before you push.
    - Rap: Wrap yourself in a towel before you get into the car.
    - Written: The letter was written with disappearing ink.
    - Gnome: Thieves stole the gnome and hid it in the shed.
    - Crum: A crumb from the cookie landed in the cup.
- Play "Word Families" with words from the word list below. Instructions can be found on page 107.
    - Example: comb — combing, recomb, recombing, combed, recombed, combable, recombable, combs

You Do — Connecting to meaning: Using the Silent Letters worksheet, follow the writing prompts using words from the word bank. This may be challenging for some students so have them create sentences orally with a partner before putting them down on paper. Do several examples together as a class if necessary. Extend the activity with your own prompts.

Word List

kn	gh	mb	wr	bt
knack	ghastly	bomb	shipwreck	debt
knead	gherkin	climb	wrap	doubt
knee	ghetto	crumb	wrath	
kneecap	ghost	dumb	wreak	**gn**
kneel	ghoul	lamb	wreath	
knew	spaghetti	limb	wren	design
knick	yoghurt	numb	write	gnarl
knife		plumb	writer	gnash
knight		plumber	written	gnat
knit/knitting		succumb	wry	gnaw
knob		tomb	wreck	gnome
knock		thumb	wrench	gnu
knoll		womb	wrist	sign
knot			wrong	
know/known			wrote	
			wrung	

Lesson 5: Vowel Teams

Description of Concept

Vowel teams are one or more letters that work together to make a vowel sound. They usually (but not always) make a long vowel sound. Vowel teams include diphthongs, which are two vowel sounds that slide from one to the other through changes in the mouth position. Vowel teams are contained in one syllable (e.g., 'oy' as in boy or 'ou' as in sound) and stay together when dividing multisyllable words into syllables. They are part of the 6 Syllable Rules (see Chapter 5).

I have found that many upper elementary/middle school students struggle with spelling vowel teams. There are many teams and some have less dependable rules or patterns than others. A good spelling assessment will guide teachers in determining which vowel teams need to be addressed through explicit instruction.

Since there are so many vowel teams, a generic lesson and word lists have been included for some of the most common vowel teams. Remember to capitalize on opportunities to review vowel teams as you encounter them in daily work and across the curriculum.

Vowel Team Word Lists

ai/ay (long ā)   oa/ow (long ō)   ee/ea (long ē)   oo (long ō)
igh (long ī)   aw/au (the sound ä)   ou (makes four sounds)

Diphthongs: oi/oy   ow/ou

I Do
- Teach the vowel team using the information included with each word list.

We Do
- Draw from the activities listed at the beginning of this chapter.
- Every time a new long vowel sound is introduced, review previous knowledge regarding long vowels. For example, as part of the introduction to vowel teams 'ai' and 'ay,' talk about the different ways that students know how to make the long ā sound. They know the letter name 'ā,' they know

Lessons 121

that an open syllable that ends in 'a' makes the long ā sound and they know that 'a'-consonant-e (magic 'e') makes the / ā / sound. Continually reviewing previous long vowel knowledge helps students make connections and builds a strong phonics foundation.
- Phoneme-grapheme spelling is very helpful when teaching vowel teams. It allows students to see that the vowel team must go in the same box as they work together to make one sound.
- Word Seekers: This would be a great review activity once you have worked with several sets of vowel teams.
- Using the word lists provided, create customized lists for practice reading as a class. Word list reading is an opportunity for students to become proficient readers of the vowel team concepts being studied.
- Use "Spelling Dictation" (page 103) to practice the spelling of these words.
- Use "Speed Drawing" (page 37) to bridge vocabulary and spelling.

You Do
- Word Sorts work well for vowel teams if students are not visually sorting words. For example, a word sort for the sounds that 'oo' makes would be an excellent sort.
- Provide opportunities for students to practice reading vowel teams in connected text. Suggestions for accessing passages can be found in Chapter 3.
- Have students write sentences and/or paragraphs using words containing the targeted vowel team.
- Draw from the activities listed at the beginning of this chapter.

Vowel Teams 'ai' and 'ay' (long ā)

The predictable vowel teams 'ai' and 'ay' make the /ā/ sound. The vowel team 'ai' is found in the middle of a word and never at the end of a word, as English words do not end in 'i.' The vowel team 'ay' is usually found at the end of a word but may appear at the beginning or middle of a word (e.g., mayor).

Word Lists: Vowel teams 'ai' and 'ay' (long ā)					
Sound-to-Symbol		'ai' Tier 1	'ai' Tier 2	'ay' Tier 1	'ay' Tier 2
'ai'	'ay'				
ail	bay	aim	ail	away	array
aim	clay	airplane	ailment	bay	assay
braid	day	braid	braille	clay	bayonet
brain	decay	brain	complaint	crayon	betray
chain	dismay	chain	contain	day	cay
detain	display	chair	dainty	daycare	decay
drain	fray	complain	detain	hay	deejay
faith	hay	drain	domain	grey/gray	delay
flail	inlay	faith	entertain	holiday	dismay
mail	may	jail	explain	layer	display
mislaid	pay	mail	flail	may	essay
nail	play	mailperson	grain	mayor	foray
plain	pray	nail	maintain	pay	fray
quail	quay	paid	mayonnaise	play	inlay
raid	relay	plain	mislaid	pray	mayonnaise
repair	repay	quail	quaint	ray	portray
snail	spray	railway	raid	say	quay
stain	tray	raisin	reclaim	spray	relay
stair	way	snail	remainder	today	rayon
train	runway	stain	repair	tray	slay
trait	slay	stair	saint	way	splay
waif	stray	stairway	sustain		stray
wail	sway	train	trait		sway
wait		waist	waif		waylay
		wait	wail		

Vowel Teams 'oa' and 'ow' (long ō)

Of the vowel teams 'oa' and 'ow' only 'oa' is predictable to make the long 'o' sound—'ow' is not predictable. The team 'oa' is commonly found in the middle of a word and 'ow' at the end. The vowel team 'ow' also makes the /ow/ sound as in *cow* (see Dipthong 'ow' on page 127).

Word Lists: Vowel teams 'oa' and 'ow' (long ō)					
Sound-to-symbol		'oa' Tier 1	'oa' Tier 2	'ow' Tier 1	'ow' Tier 2
'oa'	'ow'	boat	approach	arrow	bellow
		coal	bloat	below	fellow
bloat	below	cocoa	boar	borrow	glow
boast	blow	float	boast	bowl	hollow
broach	bowl	goal	broach	box	meadow
cloak	box	goat	cloak	crow	mellow
coach	crow	groan	coach	flow	narrow
coal	flow	load	coast	grow	sow
coast	grow	loaf	coax	low	stow
float	low	moan	foal	mow	
goal	mow	oak	goatee	pillow	
goat	ow	oat	hoax	shadow	
groan	shadow	oatmeal	loan	show	
load	show	railroad	moan	slow	
loan	slow	road	moat	snow	
moan	snow	roast	poach	swallow	
moat	throw	sailboat	roach	throw	
roast	tow	soap	roam	willow	
soap	window	throat	soak	window	
soar		toad	soapbox	yellow	
throat		toast	soar		
toast					

Vowel Teams 'ee' and 'ea' (long ē)

The vowel teams 'ee' and 'ea' make the long /ē/ sound, as in *meet* and *meat*.

The vowel team 'ea' can also make the short ĕ sound (head), the long ā sound (steak) and when followed by 'r' makes either the /ē/ sound (fear) and /ĕ/ sound (pear). It is a tricky one but it can be helpful for students to know that the long /ē/ sound is the most common.

Word Lists: Vowel Teams 'ee' and 'ea' make the long 'e' sound /E/

'ee' Tier 1		'ee' Tier 2		'ea' Tier 1		'ea' Tier 2	
agree	green	breed	seer	appear	leap	appeal	teak
agreed	greet	bungee	sheen	bead	meal	beacon	teal
asleep	jeep	deem	sheer	beak	mean	beagle	veal
beef	need	fleet	sleet	bean	near	beam	
beehive	peek	greed	steel	cheap	neat	bleak	
beeswax	queen	heed	steep	cheat	read	creak	
been	seed	jeer	thee	cleat	real	easel	
beep	seem	keen	teem	cream	seal	gear	
beer	seen	leek	veer	deal	seat	gleam	
beetle	sheep	leer	weep	dear	speak	heap	
between	sheet	meek		dream	spear	mead	
cheek	sleep	peer		eat	steal	peak	
cheer	steer	preen		eaten	steam	peat	
coffee	sweet	redeem		fear	team	plead	
creek	teen	reed		flea	tear	pleat	
deer	tree	reef		heal	treat	reap	
feed	weed	reem		hear	weak	seam	
	week	reek		heat	wheat	sear	
	wheel	seek		lead		shear	
				leak			

'ea' short /ĕ/
bread, breakfast, breath, dead, deaf, dread, head, health, lead, meant, read, spread, sweat, thread, threaten, wealth

'ea' long /ā/
break, great, steak

Vowel Team 'oo' Makes Four Sounds

The vowel team 'oo' makes four different sounds: /ü/ as in *book*, /ö/ as in *pool*, /ō/ as in *floor* (the vowel controlled /or/ sound), and /ŭ/ as in *flood*. It can be helpful for students to know that the sound /ö/ as in *pool* is the most common.

Word Lists: Vowel Team 'oo'

/ö/ as in pool			/ ü / as in book		/ ō / as in floor	/ ŭ / as in flood
baboon	gloom	scoop	book	stood	door	blood
balloon	mood	shoot	brook	took	floor	flood
bamboo	moon	smooth	cook	understood	moor	
bloom	pool	spook	crook	wood	poor	
broom	proof	spoon	foot	wool		
boot	roof	soon	good			
cartoon	room	stool	hood			
cool	root	too	hook			
doom	saloon	tool	look			
drool		tooth	rook			
fool		zoo	shook			
food		zoom				

Lessons 125

Trigraph 'igh'

Trigraphs are three letters that combine to make one new sound. The trigraph 'igh' makes the long /ī/ sound. It is often followed by the letter 't.' There are only four 'igh' words that are not followed by a 't' (high, nigh, sigh, thigh).

Word List: Vowel team 'igh' (long i)		
blight	light	sight
bright	midnight	sightsee
fight	might	slight
fright	nigh	thigh
frighten	night	tight
high	plight	tighten
highlight	right	tonight
highway	sigh	uptight

Vowel Teams 'aw' and 'au'

The vowel teams 'aw' and 'au' make the sound ä, as in *saw* and *haul*. 'Au' can be found at the beginning and middle of words, but never at the end, since English words never end in 'u.' 'Aw' can be found at the beginning, middle, and end of words (awful, drawl, law).

Word List: Vowel teams 'aw' and 'au' (ä)						
aw			au		al	wa
awesome	fawn	saw	applaud	gauntlet	alder	narwal
awful	hawk	scrawl	audit	haul	all	swab
awning	jaw	scrawny	August	haunch	appall	swamp
bawl	jigsaw	shawl	aunt	haunt	also	swan
claw	law	slaw	astronaut	jaunt	alto	swap
crawfish	lawn	spawn	author	laud	always	swat
crawl	outlaw	squawk	because	launch	bald	wad
dawn	paw	straw	cauldron	laundry	balm	waffle
draw	pawn	thaw	cause	maul	call	waft
drawl	prawn	yaw	clause	nautical	calm	walk
flaw	raw	withdraw	dinosaur	pause	halt	wall
	rawhide		exhaust	sauna	malt	wan
			fault	trauma	palm	want
			fraud	vault	salsa	wash
					tall	wasp
						water

Vowel team 'ou'

'Ou', as in *ouch*, is a diphthong, and it is the most common use of the vowel team 'ou.' 'Ou' can also make four other sounds. With these sounds, 'ou' is no longer a diphthong but works as a vowel team because the two vowels make a single sound:

- /ō/ as in *soul*
- /ö/ as in *group*
- /ü/ as in *could*
- /ŭ/ as in *country*

'Ou' can be used at the beginning and in the middle of a word, but never at the end because no English word ends in 'u.'

Word Lists: Vowel team 'ou'					
/ō/ as in soul		/ö/ as in group		/ü/ as in could	/ ŭ / as in country
amour	mourn	coup	recoup	could	couple
boulder	poultry	coupon	route	should	cousin
court	pour	contour	soup	would	country
four	shoulder	croup	tour		double
fourth	soul	detour	tourist		doubly
gourd	your	doula	velour		touch
gourmet		group	wound		trouble
		ghoul	you		young
		mousse	youth		

Diphthongs 'oi' and 'oy'

Diphthongs are two vowel sounds that slide from one to the other through changes in the mouth position. The diphthongs 'oi' and 'oy' make the same sound ('oi' as in boil and 'oy' as in destroy). Diphthong 'oi' is most commonly found at the beginning and in middle of words because English words do not end in 'i.' 'Oy' is most commonly found at the end of a word, but it can also be found at the beginning and middle of a word.

Word Lists: vowel teams 'oi' and 'oy'					
sound-to-symbol		'oi' Simple Concepts		'oy' Simple Concepts	'oy' Complex Concepts
'oi'	'oy'				
boil	boy	avoid	poison	ahoy	annoy
coil	coy	broil	spoil	decoy	employee
coin	joy	droid	toilet	deploy	gargoyle
foil	ploy	embroil	void	destroy	voyeur
join	soy	foil		employer	
koi	toy	hoist		enjoy	
oil		joint		loyal	
soil		moist		oyster	
toil		noise		royal	
void		oink			
		point			

Diphthongs 'ow' and 'ou'

The diphthong 'ow' can make two different sounds—the /ō/ sound as in *row* and 'ow' as in *cow*. This lesson focuses on the latter sound, /ow/ as in *cow*.

The diphthong 'ou' as in *ouch* is the most common use of 'ou,' but it can also make four other sounds, as in the words *soul, group, country,* and *could*.

'Ou' can be used at the beginning and in the middle of a word, but never at the end because no English word ends in 'u.'

Word Lists: diphthongs 'ow' and 'ou'						
ow **Sound-to-Symbol/Tier 1**		**ow** **Tier 2**	**ou** **Sound-to-Symbol/Tier 1**		**ou** **Tier 2**	
bow	power	allow	about	noun	abound	mound
brown	shower	brow	aloud	ouch	amount	mount
clown	sow	browse	around	our	astound	pouch
crowd	towel	browser	cloud	out	bound	pout
crown	tower	chowder	couch	outfit	bout	rout
down	town	cowl	count	pound	clout	scout
flower	vow	dowel	flour	proud	compound	shroud
frown	vowel	drown	found	round	counselor	snout
growl		empower	grouch	shout	crouch	spout
how		fowl	ground	sound	foul	stout
now		howl	house	sour	gout	trout
owl		jowl	loud	south	grout	wound
plow		prowl	mouse		hound	
pow		scowl	mouth		lout	

Vowel-r

Vowel-r (also known as vowel controlled 'r' or "bossy 'r'") is called "vowel controlled" because the 'r' impacts the vowel before it. Rather than make its long or short sound, the vowel makes a new sound. Although there are five vowel-controlled spellings (ar, er, ir, or, ur), there are only three pronunciations: /ar/ as in *barn*, /or/ as in *corn* and /er/ as in *bird, fern, curl*. Vowel-r is considered one of the 6 Syllable Rules because it stays together as a team when dividing multisyllable words into syllables.

'ar': When teaching vowel-r, 'ar' is a good team to start with because students like that it makes the sound of a pirate, argh! 'Ar' can occur at the beginning (**ar**ticle), middle (d**ar**t) or end of a word (f**ar**).

'or': 'Or' makes the /or/ sound as in sport, worn and port but in some dialects it can take on the /er/ sound. In my region, the words minor and worthy are pronounced as /miner/ and /werthy/. Another distinctive of 'or' is that when a word describing a person or progession has a Latin root 'or' is used instead of 'er' (e.g., tutor, doctor).

'er', 'ur' and 'ir': These three vowel-r teams make the sound /er/. 'Er', 'ur', and 'ir' words are easy to read but they can be quite difficult to spell because there is no rule to guide students when they are spelling a word with the /er/ sound. One helpful hint is that 'er' is the most common, followed by 'ur' and finally 'ir'. If students are unsure of the correct spelling, this knowledge can help them make a knowledgeable choice, rather than guessing.

ar	or	er	ir	ur
afterward, alarm, apartment, apparel, apparently, arcade, arch, ark, arm, army, art, artist, barn, backward, barge, bark, bombard, burglar, calendar, car, carpenter, carpet, cart, carton, carve, charm, chart, custard, dark, darling, dart, depart, discard, far, farm, farmer, forward, garden, gargle, garlic, hard, harm, harp, harvest, jar, large, lizard, lunar, marble, march, margin, market, mustard, nectar, orchard, paragraph, pardon, part, partner, party, polar, preparation, scar, scarf, scarlet, shark, sharp, smart, solar, spar, sparkle, standard, star, start, starve, tar, tarnish, tarp, tart, transparency, upward, vicar, wizard, yard, yarn	acorn, actor, born, chord, cord, cork, corn, doctor, dorm, emperor, factor, floor, for, ford, forgot, fork, form, fort, forty, glory, gory, horn, hornet, horrid, horror, horse, lord, major, memory, minor, norm, north, odor, or, organ, orbit, pastor, porch, pork, port, razor, resort, sailor, short, snort, sort, sport, stork, storm, story, tenor, torch, torn, thorn, tutor, worn	after, berg, eastern, enter, ever, expert, faster, fern, finger, flower, germ, her, herd, jerk, kernel, lantern, mixer, nerd, nerve, never, northern, over, pattern, perch, perfect, perfume, person, river, serve, sister, slower, stern, southern, swerve, tower, verb, verse, western, whisper	bird, birch, birth, birthday, blackbird, chirp, confirm, dirt, fir, firm, first, flirt, girl, girth, irk, quirk, shirt, sir, skirt, smirk, squirm, squirt, stir, swirl, third, thirst, thirteen, twirl, whirl	burger, burn, burlap, burp, burst, church, churn, curb, curl, curse, curt, curve, disturb, fur, further, hurt, lurk, murky, nurse, nurture, purple, purse, return, slur, slurp, spur, spurt, sunburn, surf, surprise, Thursday, turd, turf, turn, turtle, yurt
Exceptions				
dollar, marry	tailor, tractor, word, work, worm			

Lessons 6A and 6B: Hard and Soft c and g

Although the rule, or pattern, is the same for hard and soft 'c' and 'g,' they are broken into two lessons to enable students to focus on one concept at a time. This is especially helpful because this pattern is less reliable with 'g'. Older students, or those that may have had exposure to this rule, may be able to work with hard and soft 'c' and 'g' at the same time.

Hard and Soft 'c'
Materials needed:
- Lesson plan
- Word list to project

Lessons

- Texts with hard and soft "c" (West Viriginia phonics and UFLI)
- Worksheet for sorting hard and soft 'c' words
- Phoneme-grapheme grids

The Rule:
- When 'c' is followed by 'e,' 'i,' or 'y,' it makes a soft 'c' sound /s/ (e.g., cider, concept, pounce).
- When 'c' is followed by 'a,' 'u' and 'o' (or no letter), it makes a hard 'c' sound /k/ (e.g., coffee, canteloupe, electric).
- This is a fairly reliable rule.

I Do
- Teach your students the following concepts.
- Beginning readers are often taught that the letter 'c' makes the /k/ sound when, in reality, 'c' makes two sounds: /k/ as in *cut* and /s/ as in *cider*. The rule determining which sound is made is simple and quite reliable:
When 'c' is followed by 'a,' 'o,' or 'u,' it makes the /k/ sound.
When it is followed 'e', 'i,' or 'y,' it makes the /s/ sound.
- Young students can remember this concept by singing the following song, set to the tune of BINGO:
    There are 3 letters that soften "c," E-I-E-I-Y.
    The same 3 often soften "g," E-I-E-I-Y.
While it is a silly little song, I often can get older students to sing this song with me because they realize that by setting the rule to music, it helps them remember the concept and the three vowels that are involved in manipulating the sound of 'c.'
- Provide examples of words that follow the rule and those that do not (draw words from the word lists below). Examples might include the following:
Follow the rule: cinder, place, sincere, excite, fancy
Do not follow the rule: cello, soccer, Caesar, facade

We Do
- There are two word reading lists included for this lesson. **List A** is composed of words suitable for more advanced readers while **List B** is composed of words that use simpler phonics concepts. Project a word list with either a projector or document camera.
- Read the word list of choice together as a class. Stop and talk about some of the definitions of words that are new to the class. Reread the word list at a steady pace, now that the words are more familiar to students. Ask if there are any students who would like to try reading the list on their own. Remind them not to rush but to read at the rate of speaking.
- Have students come up and underline the 'ce,' 'ci,' 'cy' words. Remove the projected words and using graph paper and "Phoneme-Grapheme Spelling," (page 101), spell list words together on the graph paper. Emergent spellers should be able to participate as the work is done together as a class with the teacher modeling each word.

You Do
- Use word sort **worksheets** for hard and soft 'c.' Worksheet A has some complex words. Students will need to decide what to do with words that contain both a hard and soft 'c,' which could generate interesting conversation.
- Have students play "50/50" with words taken from the word lists.

- Do "Spelling Dictation" (page 103) with 10–12 words from the word lists. Create a simple phrase or sentence for each word and have students write them in their notebooks/binders. Phrases might include the following: an ear of corn, I like to climb, three pink mice, in the center, white cotton, a small cardinal, sweet cider, you can decide, meet me at recess, a good citizen, a sharp pencil, a star in space.
- Provide a text paragraph with hard and soft 'c' and 'g' words. Ask students to find the hard and soft 'c's and circle or underline them. See Passage Reading on page 34 for sources of passages. The following passage from *National Geographic Kids* would work well: https://www.natgeokids.com/uk/discover/science/nature/water-cycle/. The following is an example of a passage generated on the decodable text generator from Project Read (page 34).

> Once upon a time, in a spicy city, a circus had set up its center. Thea, a small girl, was excited. She saw a fancy cycle with a lacy seat. Next, she saw a cinnamon stall. She gave a cent to get a cinnamon stick. Then, she saw a stand selling icicles. They were as cold as acid but very tasty. After that, she saw a princess, who was practicing to recite a poem. She had a pencil and a stencil to write it down. At the end of the day, the circus made Thea feel like she was in a magical circle of joy. She went home and dreamt of the circus city that night.

Word List: Hard 'c'		
sound-to-symbol	**simple concepts**	**complex concepts**
cabin cord corn crab drastic panic music **simple magic 'e'** cake cape clove	Atlantic cabinet calculate candle cardinal carnival carry climb cobble combine complete cotton cracker cursive electric hectic object uncle	candle carousel caustic conductor country cursive project
Exceptions to the rule		Caesar

Word List: Soft 'c'			
acid cent city pencil **simple magic 'e'** face fence ice lice mice space trace wince	celery cell cemetery center centipede cider cinder circumstance citrus distance decide entrance extravagance	fancy lettuce incident innocent peace place price process recess reference sincere	certain cigarette citizen cylinder cyst excite flounce juice pounce prophecy science voice
Exceptions to the rule:		arcing façade indict soccer	
Words that include hard and a soft 'c': accent, accept/acceptable, bicycle, Celtic, circus, concert, condolence, cyclops, Pacific, vaccine			

Word List A

cinder	pricey	fence	excite	center	century	dance
citrus	cellular	thrice	pencil	cyber	stance	cyclone
caustic	cyst					

Word List B

ice	cinder	price	cast	cube	race	center
cell	acid	fancy	dance	rice	citrus	fence
city						

Note 1: There are many words in the above lists that will be new vocabulary for students. Choose a balance of words where students know the meaning and those that will contribute to vocabulary building

Note 2: Magic 'e' words have been added to the sound-to-symbol list since this concept was taught in Lesson 3.

Hard and Soft 'g'

There are several spellings that seem unusual but make sense because of the hard and soft 'g' rule. For example, when adding the ending *-able* to a word that ends in 'ge,' the 'e' is retained to keep the soft /j/ sound (judgeable, cagey).

When "borrowing" words from other languages, as English often does, there are times when a silent letter is inserted to protect the hard 'g' sound because it is followed by 'e,' 'i,' or 'y.' In Italian words, an 'h' is inserted to separate the 'g' and the 'e' (ghetto, spaghetti). In French and Spanish words, a silent 'u' is inserted to separate the 'g' from 'e' and 'i' and retain the hard 'g' sound (guide, plague, guerilla, guitar).

The Rule

- Hard 'g' says /g/.
- Soft 'g' says /j/.
- When 'g' is followed by 'e,' 'i,' or 'y', it makes a soft 'g' sound (e.g., giant, fudge).
- When 'g' is followed by 'a,' 'u,' or 'o' (or no letter), it makes a hard 'g' sound (e.g., gopher, gallop).
- This rule is not as reliable as that of hard and soft 'c.' There are times when 'g' retains its hard sound even when followed by 'e,' 'i,' or 'y' (e.g., get, girl).

I Do
- Hard 'g' says /g/ and soft 'g' says /j/.
- Review the hard and soft 'c' rule from the previous lesson and explain that the same vowels will soften 'g.'
- Demonstrate with words from the word list below.
- Sing the song if appropriate.
- This is less predictable than the hard and soft 'c' phonics rule. There are times when 'g' retains its hard sound even when followed by 'e,' 'i,' or 'y' (get, girl, margarine).

We Do
- Read words from the lists below and after reading each word, have students indicate whether they are hearing a hard or soft 'g.' Read a word like *orange* and the students say either /g/ or /j/. You could also have them say 'hard g' or 'soft g.' If you find you need to practice this over several days, have them say the sound they hear one day and indicate whether it is hard 'g' or soft 'g' the next.
- Challenge students by adding a few words where both sounds are present (e.g., engage, garbage, language). These words are included in the following word list. Challenge them further by adding hard and soft 'c' words as well.
- Write the word *engage* on the board. Explain that the final **sound** in it is /j/. Ask students why it is not spelled 'engaj.' No English word ends in 'j' so this is a clue that when they are spelling, if the final sound is /j/ they must use 'ge.'
- Project a list of words onto the board and read the list together. Choose words that are appropriate for your students. Add exceptions and some nonsense words to support a solid identification of the concept.
- Extend this activity by having students come up to the board and circle the soft 'g's and underline the hard 'g's. They can also come up and lead by pointing to a variety of words in random order, which the class must read aloud together.

- Post the same list over several days and time the choral reading of the list to see if they can get faster as the week progresses. Students must stay together as a group to achieve a time. Review words that they find tricky or tend to slow down for. Remind them that the goal is to read at the rate of speech, so no rushing!
- Some emergent readers will struggle with the choral readings but being in the room for the lesson and hearing their peers read the list can still be beneficial.
- Using graph paper and "Phoneme-Grapheme Spelling" (page 101), spell list words together on the graph paper. Emergent spellers should be able to participate as the work is done together as a class.

You Do

- Provide a paragraph with hard and soft 'c' and 'g' words. Students must find the hard and soft *c*'s and *g*'s (circle and underline). See Passage Reading on page 34 for sources of passages
- Create a **word sort** and copy cards onto cardstock or manila tags. Scaffold your sorts by using easy-to-read words in one deck and more challenging words in another. (I copy the two different sorts on different colors of card stock, so I know which is which.) Have students sort the words into hard and soft 'g' words or piles. Sorts can be done with a paper/pencil worksheet, but it is much more engaging for students to do this work in a multimodal activity. If you have non-readers or early emergent readers, use pictures of words that contain hard and soft 'g' and have them identify if the sound is hard or soft 'g' for the sort.
- Do Spelling Dictation (page 103) with 10–12 words from the word lists. Create a sentence or phrase with each word and have students write them in their notebooks/binders. Check for correct spelling of target words as well as punctuation. Phrases might include: go to the gym, a new judge, the large fish, white as a ghost, the egg cracked, the brown gopher, lack of energy, do not giggle, soon we will begin, the gelatin is orange, I like ginger ale, do not divulge secrets, the story is tragic, and let's eat some fudge.
- Using their notebooks/binders for writing, ask students to choose five each of hard and soft 'g' and 'c' words (10 total) and add affixes to them. Here are some examples:
    accept: unacceptable, unaccepting, accepted, accepts, reaccepts, reaccept, unaccept, unaccepts
    charge: charging, charged, chargeable, recharge, unchargeable, recharging

The following lists are examples of lists sorted by Tier 1 and 2 vocabulary. You can mix hard and soft 'c' and 'g' words once 'g' has been explicitly taught and practiced.

Word List for Hard and Soft 'g'				
Tier 1				Tier 2
Hard 'g'		Soft 'g'	Hard 'g'	Soft 'g'
alligator	goat	cage	cardigan	badge
begun	golf	change	catalogue	divulge
bragging	gone	engine	configure	gelatin
danger	good	fridge	dagger	gentleman
drag	goodness	fudge	disgust	geography
dragon	goose	gem	garter	germ
egg	got	gentle	gasp	gesture
energy	graduation	gerbil	gavel	ginger
game	grand	giant	glimmer	gymnasium
gap	grandma	gin	glint	hinge
gather	grandpa	giraffe	globe	ledge
germ	great	gym	gopher	lunge
get	green	huge	gosling	origin
ghost	grin	judge	gradual	rage
glass	grip	large	graft	salvage
glitter	leg	orange	gravel	selvedge
glow	rug	page	grime	tragic
		stage	gulf	urgent
		stranger	gull	vegetable
			gurgle	verge
			migration	
			progress	
			smog	

Words that contain both hard and soft 'g': baggage, engage, gadget, garage, garbage, gauge, geography, ginseng, gorge, grudge, grunge, language, pilgrimage

Exceptions: anger, argyle, begin, beige, bigger, biology, gear, get, gift, giggle, gill, girl, give, hunger, linger, longer, margarine, trigger

Lesson 7: Complex Consonants

Often called a complex consonant, 'tch' and 'dge' are trigraphs—three letters that make one sound. These are commonly misspelled patterns that can be corrected with explicit instruction.

The Pattern Rule

When a short vowel is followed by 'ch,' a silent letter 't' is inserted between the short vowel and the digraph to protect the short vowel (e.g., hutch, watch, catch). The same rule applies when a short vowel is followed by 'ge'; a silent letter 'd' is inserted between the short vowel and 'ge' to protect the short vowel (e.g., fudge, ledge, grudge).

This rule is often called the soldier rule because the silent letters 't' and 'd' act as a soldier on duty. Soldiers 't' and 'd' are not needed if there is a letter between the short vowel and 'ch' and 'ge' (e.g., lunch, range) or if there is vowel team that makes the long vowel sound long (e.g., peach, siege).

The use of 'ck' also follows this rule. While many students simply put a 'c' before the 'k' at the end of a word, the soldier rule is at work. In a single syllable word, if the vowel is short, followed by a 'k,' a soldier 'c' is required (e.g., chick). If the vowel is long or a consonant is between the short vowel and the 'k,' a 'c' is not required (e.g., peak, trunk).

This lesson can be divided into two parts depending on the skills and needs of your class. If dividing the lesson, teach 'tch' and then reteach the lesson with 'dge.'

The Rule:

When a short vowel is followed by 'ch,' a silent letter "t" is inserted between the short vowel and the digraph to protect the short vowel (e.g., hutch, watch, catch). The same rule applies when a short vowel is followed by 'ge'; a silent letter 'd' is inserted between the short vowel and 'ge' to protect the short vowel (e.g., fudge, ledge, grudge).

I Do:
- The tomb of the unknown soldier is at the National War Memorial in Ottawa. The tomb contains the remains of an unknown Canadian Soldier who fought and died in France during WW1. Sentries stand guard at the tomb to show Canada's commitment to remember and honour Canadians who served in war. There is a similar memorial for Canadians and other Commonwealth countries at Westminster Abbey in London and a memorial for the unknown American soldier in Arlington Cemetery in Virginia. Nathan Cirrillo was a Canadian Soldier who was killed at the Canadian National War Memorial in Ottawa in 2014.
- Engage students in a conversation on why soldiers do not talk when they are on duty (to not be distracted and to stay focused on the job). I sometimes refer to the guards at Buckingham Palace for this part of the lesson as many students know that they do not speak when on duty.
- Explain that when a short vowel is followed by 'ch,' a silent letter 't' is inserted between the short vowel and the digraph to protect the short vowel (e.g., hutch, watch, catch). The same rule applies when a short vowel is followed by 'ge'; a silent letter 'd' is inserted between the short vowel and 'ge' to protect the short vowel (e.g., fudge, ledge, grudge).
- This rule is often called the soldier rule because the silent letters 't' and 'd' act as a soldier on duty (as per the discussion above). Soldiers 't' and 'd' are not needed if there is a letter between the short vowel and 'tch' and 'dge' or if there is vowel team which makes a long vowel sound (e.g., peach, siege).
- Review the 'ck' pattern showing how 'ck' also follows the soldier pattern rule.

We Do
- For this concept, **phoneme-grapheme** spelling is very helpful for students. It allows them to see that the trigraphs 'tch' and 'dge' must go in the same box as they make one sound.
- Use "Spelling Dictation" (page 103) to practice the spelling of these words.
- Games like "Wordle," "Connections," "Is It Spelled Correctly?" and "It's Up to You!" all work well when teaching this concept. When asking students if a word is spelled correctly, include 'tch' and 'dge' along with words that do not require the soldier because the vowel is long or there is a vowel team.

You Do   Choose from one or more of the activities below.
- Use the Spelling BINGO concept (page 107).
- Word sorts do not work well for this concept as words can be visually sorted without reading.
- Use short passages that include multiple examples of 'tch' and 'dge' words.
- Ask students to choose 6–8 of the list words and write sentences or a meaningful paragraph that includes these words.

Word Lists for 'tch' and 'dge'					
Tier 1 - tch	**Tier 2 - tch**		**Tier 1 - dge**	**Tier 2 - dge**	
birdwatching	backstitch	outstretched	badge	abridge	partridge
butcher	batch	pitchfork	bridge	acknowledge	pledge
butterscotch	bewitch	potlatch	dodge	badger	porridge
catch	blotch	ratchet	edge	bludgeon	ridge
chitchat	britches	retch	fridge	budge	ridgeline
ditch	catchall	satchel	fudge	budget	ridgepole
fetch	catchment	Scotch/scotch	headgear	cartridge	selvedge
gotcha	catchy	sketchy	hedgehog	codger	sludge
hopscotch	clutch	snatch	judge	curmudgeon	smidge
itch	crochet	snitch	lodge	dislodge	smidgen
ketchup	crosshatch	splotch		drawbridge	straightedge
kitchen	crutch	stretcher		dredge	trudge
match	dispatch	stitch/stitchery		drudge/	unabridged
patch	dispatcher	swatch		drudgery	wedge
pitch	etch	switchback		fidget	widgeon
pitcher	fetching	switchboard		fledge	widget
scratch	glitch	switcheroo		gadget	
sketch	hatch	thatch		grudge	
stopwatch	hatchback	topstitch		hedgerow	
stretch	hatchery	twitch		hodgepodge	
switch	hatchet	watchtower		judgement/	
watch	hatchling	witchcraft		judgment	
watchdog	hitch/hitchhike	wretch		knowledge	
witch	hutch	wretched		ledge	
wristwatch	latch			ledger	
	latchkey			lodge/lodger	
	matchbook			midget	
	mismatch			misjudge	
	notch			nudge	

Lesson 8: Consonant-le

The Rule:
Consonant-le (C-le) works as a team to create one syllable. It is found at the end of multisyllable words. Although the 'e' is silent, it holds the place of the vowel since every syllable contains a written vowel (or vowel team). A schwa sound is inserted between the consonant and the 'l' and makes the /əl/ sound, which sounds like /ŭl/ (e.g., subtle, maple, example).

Consonant-le is one of the 6 Syllable Rules and is an important rule for both reading and writing.

Reading Consonant-le
This is an important reading rule as it impacts whether the syllable before it is read as open or closed. The reader must count back three letters (C-le) to see the syllable that is before it.

$$\begin{array}{c} \text{m a p l e} \\ \text{3 2 1} \end{array}$$

$$\begin{array}{c} \text{m a } | \text{ p l e} \\ \text{3 2 1} \end{array}$$

In the word *maple*, the division is between the 'a' and the 'p.' This makes the first syllable 'ma,' which is an open syllable so the vowel is pronounced as a long ā – /A/.

$$\begin{array}{c} \text{d i m p l e} \\ \text{3 2 1} \end{array}$$

$$\begin{array}{c} \text{d i m } | \text{ p l e} \\ \text{3 2 1} \end{array}$$

In the word *dimple*, the division is between the 'm' and the 'p.' This makes the first syllable 'dim' a closed syllable so the vowel is pronounced as a short ĭ – /i/.

I have often worked with students who did not understand this rule. In these cases, students pronounce *bugle* as bug-gle because they do not know how to divide the word into syllables recognizing the role of C-le.

Spelling Consonant-le
Since consonant-le has a voiced schwa between the consonant and the 'l' it can be tricky from a spelling perspective. Students who are carefully breaking words down by sounds (phonemes) will tend to write words like *handle* as 'handul,' which is what they hear.

If a multisyllable word ends in the /ŭl/ sound, that is a cue that consonant-le is probably at work.

Weird Bits and Exceptions
'ckle': The letter team 'ckle' is a unique "work around" for the rule that 'c' and 'k' cannot be doubled in the middle of a word. To create a short vowel when the first syllable of a consonant-le word ends in the sound /k/, use 'ckle.' When students see 'ckle,' their best strategy is to identify the base word as the first syllable and then add 'kle' for the second syllable (pick in pickle and buck in buckle). This is not to be confused with the soldier rule of silent c in 'ck.'

$$\begin{array}{c} \text{p i c k l e} \\ \text{3 2 1} \end{array}$$

$$\begin{array}{c} \text{p i c } | \text{ k l e} \\ \text{3 2 1} \end{array}$$

pronounced pick-kle

'tle': When students see the letter team 'tle' it is an alert to the fact that the 't' may be silent (e.g., whistle, castle). Why? The reason is that these Old English words originally had a pronounced 't.' *Whistle* used to be 'whistlian' and *castle* used to be 'castel.' There is no clue as to when the silent 't' is present for spelling, so students will need to memorize this pattern.

The Rule

Consonant-le (C-le) works as a team to create one syllable. It is found at the end of multisyllable words. Although the 'e' is silent, it holds the place of the vowel since every syllable contains a vowel (or vowel team). A schwa sound is inserted between the consonant and the 'l' and makes the /əl/ sound, which sounds like /ŭl/ (e.g., subtle, maple, example).

The reader must count back three letters (C-le) at the end of the word. They will then be able to tell if the syllable before the C-le is open or closed.

I Do
- Teach consonant-le using the information above. Engage students in a discussion of words they know that follow this rule and whether they have had trouble reading and spelling it in the past.

We Do
- Read word lists of words that contain consonant-le.
- For this concept, **phoneme-grapheme** spelling is very helpful for students. It allows them to see that the consonant goes in one box and the 'le' must go in another box as they make one sound.
- Use "Spelling Dictation" (page 103) to practice the spelling of these words.

You Do Select from one or more of the strategies below.

- **Consonant-le Word Hunt worksheet** (page 144). Students may work in pairs if you have emergent and grade level readers. Note that Tier 2 words are included in the instructions for this worksheet so emergent readers may need help reading these instructions.
- This pattern is one of the 6 Syllable Rules. Look at multisyllable consonant-le words on the next page and practice breaking them into syllables.
- Choose from activities in the spelling activities listed in this chapter.

-ble	-cle	-ckle	-dle	-fle	-gle
able	article	buckle	bundle	baffle	angle
bible	bicycle	cackle	cradle	battle	bugle
babble	circle	chuckle	cuddle	muffle	dangle
bobble	cubicle	fickle	doodle	raffle	eagle
bubble	cuticle	heckle	fiddle	riffle	giggle
cable	cycle	pickle	handle	scuffle	goggle
dabble	follicle	prickle	hurdle	shuffle	google
fable	icicle	spackle	idle	sniffle	haggle
grumble	miracle	sparkle	kindle	stifle	jangle
hobble	obstacle	tackle	ladle	trifle	jingle
rumble	particle	tickle	needle	truffle	juggle
scramble	popsicle		noodle	waffle	jungle
stable	recycle		paddle	whiffle	mingle
stumble	spectacle		peddle		tangle
table	uncle		riddle		toggle
thimble	vehicle		saddle		wiggle
tumble					

-kle	-ple	-tle	-zle
ankle	apple	battle	bamboozle
crinkle	ample	bottle	bedazzle
sparkle	couple	castle	dazzle
sprinkle	cripple	cattle	drizzle
twinkle	dimple	hurtle	embezzle
	example	kettle	frazzle
	maple	little	fizzle
	people	mantle	frizzle
	pimple	riddle	grizzle
	sample	rustle	guzzle
	simple	settle	nozzle
	staple	shuttle	nuzzle
	steeple	startle	muzzle
	temple	tattle	puzzle
	triple	title	razzle
		whistle	sizzle

Lesson 9: The Greeks

Greek words are commonly found in math and science terms. There are spelling patterns that students find difficult to spell due to their Greek origins. Explicit instruction with these patterns will support both reading and spelling.

The Sound of 'ch'
The digraph 'ch' makes the /k/ sound in words of Greek origin. It can be found at the beginning, in the middle, and at the end of words, and there are many of them (e.g., anchor, echo, orchestra).

The Sound of 'ph'

'Ph' is a digraph that makes the /f/ sound. It can occur at the beginning, in the middle, or at the end of a word and is found in Greek words such as *phone*, *philosopher*, and *dolphin*.

Word Lists: 'ph' and 'ch'			
ph as /f/		ch as /k/	
alpha	phase	ache	chorus
aphid	pheasant	alchemist	Christmas
autograph	philosopher	anarchy	chromatic
digraph	philosophy	archeology	chrome
dolphin	phobia	anchor	chronic
geography	phone	architect	chronicle
gopher	phoneme	architecture	chronology
graph	photo	archive	chrysanthemum
hyphen	phrase	bronchitis	echo
lymph	physical	catechism	hierarchy
morph	physics	chameleon	lichen
orphan	sphere	chamomile	mechanical
paragraph	symphony	chaos	mocha
phantom	telegraph	character	monarch
pharmacy	telephone	charisma	orchestra
	triumph	chasm	orchid
		chemistry	psychology (any psych word)
		chiropractor	scheme
		chloroform	scholar
		chlorophyll	school
		chlorine	tech (any tech word)
		choir	zucchini
		cholesterol	
		chord	
		choreography	

The Sounds of 'y'

In words of Greek origin, 'y' is pronounced with either a short 'i' (ĭ) as in *crypt* and *system* or long 'i' (ī) as in *cyclopes* and *style*. 'Y' at the end of a word of Greek origin makes the long e (ē) sound.

'y' as a short 'i' (ĭ)	'y' as a long 'i' (ī)	'y' at the end of a word (ē)
crypt crystal cynicism cyst gym hypnosis myth/mythology nymph syllable symbol synonym system	analyze cycle cyclone cyclops enzyme hyphen python style thyroid type typhoon	biology* cemetery charity democracy fury galaxy poly symphony *any 'ology' words

Silent Letters of Note in Words of Greek Origin

Word Lists: Greek Silent Letter Teams rh, mn and pn/ps/pt

rh	mn	pn/ps/pt/
rhapsody rhetoric rheumatic rhododendron rhombus rhubarb rhyme rhythm	autumn column condemn hymn mnemonic solemn	pneumonia
		psalm pseudo psychology
		ptarmigan pterodactyl

Silent Letters: Using Words in Context

Name: _____

Using the word bank, use any word in a sentence following the instructions below. Create two sentences for each prompt.

Word Bank			
doubt	writer	wry	
wreck	wrench	plumber	thumb
yoghurt	wrestle	lamb	spaghetti
design	succumb	tomb	knight

Write a sentence using one word from the word bank and one or more colors. **Example:** The red and blue **gnome** sat on the porch.

a) _____

b) _____

Choose any word from the word bank and write a sentence where you include another word that has the same meaning as your chosen word.
Example: Wael **owed** his dad $50 so he took extra shifts at work to get out of **debt**.

a) _____

b) _____

Combine two of the word bank words in one sentence.
Example: The grave digger thought he saw a **ghost** on top of the **tomb**.

a) _____

b) _____

Write a sentence using as many silent letter words as possible.

a) _____

b) _____

Consonant-le Word Hunt

Name: _____

Word Bank

whistle	pimple	heckle	paddle
bubble	ankle	dazzle	waffles
sparkle	buckle	staple	fickle
hobble	muzzle	juggle	castle
haggle	rustle	pickle	tackle
fiddle	sniffle	crackle	ample

In the word box above, find words that meet these criteria:

1. Two consonant -*le* words that contain a double consonant (e.g., puzzle). Write a definition for one of these words.

   _____

   Definition: _____

2. Two words that contain a silent 't.' Write a definition for one of these words.

   _____

   Definition: _____

3. Two words where the first syllable ends in a /k/ sound. Write a definition for one of these words.

   _____

   Definition: _____

Break the following words into syllables:

embezzle   spectacle   doodle   example

Word Sort for Hard and Soft 'c'

Name: _____

The Rule for Spelling and Reading
- 'C' makes the soft /s/ sound when it is followed by 'e,' 'i,' or 'y.'
- It makes the hard /k/ sound when it is followed by 'a,' 'u,' and 'o' (or no letter).
- This is a predictable rule.

Instructions: Sort the following word bank into hard and soft 'c.'

acid	Pacific	concert	fence
caustic	object	peace	process
hectic	gigantic	cyclone	sincere
bicycle	panic	science	circus
drastic	electric	carousel	extravagance

Hard 'c'	Soft 'c'

Word Sort for Hard and Soft 'c' (Version B)

Name: _____

The Spelling and Reading Rule
- 'C' makes the soft /s/ sound when it is followed by 'e', 'i', or 'y.'
- It makes the hard /k/ sound when it is followed by 'a', 'u,' and 'o,' or no letter.
- This is a predictable rule.

Instructions: Sort the following word bank into hard and soft 'c.'

acid	carry	circus	peace
cotton	music	citrus	pencil
juice	combine	Pacific	climb
certain	place	cemetery	bicycle
electric	decide	ounce	panic

Hard 'c'	Soft 'c'

5

Multisyllable Words

When students struggle with spelling short words, it is easy to assume that they will not be able to break down and read multisyllable words, but that is not necessarily the case. Short Tier 1 words most often have an Anglo-Saxon origin that makes them difficult to decode. While many were originally spoken the way they are spelled, over time pronunciations have changed, leaving the reader with complex spelling patterns that are difficult to decode.

Multisyllable words often come from Latin or Greek and are easier to decode. Teaching morphology will support this work as students begin to see meaningful word chunks (morphemes) and learn how to break words down into small decodable pieces.

It is worth the time to teach decoding of multisyllable words. In doing so, you can review key spelling concepts for struggling readers and reinforce the "why" of their use and purpose for strong readers. Often struggling readers and spellers are afraid of longer words—working with the patterns that follow will give them the confidence to look at the construction of words and attempt to decode them.

The 6 Syllable Rules

The 6 Syllable Rules, which support the breakdown of multisyllable words into syllables, are a good way to address phonics for upper elementary/middle school students. In *This is How We Teach Reading*, my co-author and I addressed phonics concepts and noted the 6 Syllable Rules as they appeared in our scope and sequence. This chapter addresses teaching the 6 Syllable Rules specifically.

While this chapter might seem like the place to start when working with your students in explicit reading instruction, you will see that the knowledge of how to break down multisyllable words requires an understanding of several foundational phonics concepts. You may need to teach these foundational concepts either before teaching how to breakdown multisyllable words or teach them as you move through each rule.

What Are the 6 Syllable Rules?

At the core of decoding multisyllable words is deciding what to do with the vowel. Should the vowel be pronounced as long or short? The following phonics concepts or "rules" determine their pronunciation.

---

6 Syllable Rules

1. Open syllables: ro-bot/o-pen
2. Closed syllables: fan/repin
3. Magic 'e': late/insane
4. Vowel teams: mail/show/soapbox/repeat
5. Vowel-r: art/chirp/corner/burger/sharp
6. Consonant-le: apple/temple/bubble/stable

Foundational Knowledge for Working with Multisyllable Words

There are foundational concepts that support the work of decoding multisyllable words. As you look through the list below, teach or review any concept that your students have not mastered. I consider both accuracy and automaticity when deciding if students need further instruction or simply more practice with a concept.

1. Every syllable must have a vowel.
2. Keep digraphs and blends together—this is a chance to review digraphs and blends. See Digraph and Blend review below.
3. Open and closed syllables (Ch. 4, Spelling, Lesson 1, page 110).
4. Vowel Teams (Ch. 4, Spelling, Lesson 5, page 121).
5. Consonant-le phonics pattern (Ch. 4, Spelling, Lesson 8, page 137).
6. Bases and Affixes (Ch. 3, Morphology, Lesson 1, page 66)

Digraphs and Blends Review

Blends are two- or three-consonant combinations that consistently appear together in words, but each letter retains its own sound. Examples of two-letter consonant blends include br – *bread*, gl – *glue*, sp – *spell*, dr – *drive*, fl – *float*, cl – *clamp*, st – *first*, and nd – *send*. Examples of three-letter consonant blends include scr – *script*, spl – *split*, str – *string*.

Many people ask why we teach blends in the early grades, since each letter makes its own sound. This is the moment where the teaching of blends comes into play, as blends cannot be separated when breaking down multisyllable words. Examples of blends in multisyllable words include com-**plex**, ab-**str**act and pr**ank**-**st**er. Because blends must stay together, you cannot create syllable divisions like comp-lex or abs-tract.

What Is this CVC, CCVC, CVCCVC Stuff?

Sometimes you will see this type of coding when teaching students to decode. The V stands for vowel and the C for consonant. The word *shop* would be coded

CCVC: Consonant-Consonant-Vowel-Consonant. Intensive intervention programs and some classroom programs suggest teaching students this coding to recognize spelling patterns such as vowel teams and blends.

I find that decoding of multisyllable words in upper elementary can be done without this type of coding at the classroom level. In my practice, I simply talk about consonants, vowels, blends, and vowel teams. I find coding adds more confusion than clarity, unless students have been using it from the beginning of their reading instruction. The activities that follow do not use this type of coding, but you will see it in some other programs and activities.

Syllabication

Listed below are the general steps to decode multisyllable rules:

1. Remove all affixes. If the word is *reconstructed*, remove 're' and 'ed'. This is morphology work (see Chapter 3).
2. Label the vowels.
3. Look at what is between the vowels.
4. Depending on the consonant pattern, use Animal Strategies (below) to identify the pattern OR match the consonant pattern to the animal pattern and divide accordingly.
5. Read each syllable and then blend the syllables to read the word.
6. If the pronunciation is not a word that you know, check for schwa in the unaccented syllables (often the second syllable). Apply schwa and read each syllable and blend to read the word.

The Animal Strategies

One popular way to work with multisyllable words is by using animal names as anchor points for spelling patterns. The association of a pattern with an animal helps students to remember how multisyllable words can be broken down for easy decoding. As always, a strategy like this provides independence for learners as it gives them a strategy to fall back on when they are stuck or unsure.

The Animal Patterns

Rabbit (rab-bit) or **walrus** (wal-rus): Syllables are divided between two consonants in the middle of two vowels. Again, knowledge of blends comes into effect here as you would not divide between the 'p' and 'l' in *replay* because 'pl' is a blend.

Tiger/Camel (ti-ger or cam-el): When there is one consonant between two vowels, it can either be divided before the consonant (ti-ger), creating an open syllable for the first syllable, or after the consonant (cam-el) creating a closed syllable for the first syllable.

Lion (li-on): Syllables are divided between two vowels that are **not** a vowel team.

Turtle (tur-tle): The Turtle rule is the consonant-le phonics rule at work. Consonant-le is found at the end of multisyllable words and must be kept together. The silent 'e' is the vowel for this syllable, even though it is unvoiced.

When applying the Animal rules, consonant blends count as one consonant.

Note About Graphics and Material: When using animal graphics for teaching these rules, be sure to use age-appropriate images. There is a significant amount of material available online that is too 'cutesy' for upper elementary students.

☑

☒

Freepik.com

Teaching Syllabication

If you are teaching Grades 4/5 or if you have many struggling readers, I recommend teaching each pattern in a separate lesson. While the Rabbit rule is quite simple, each concept gets progressively more challenging, and each lesson contains many Tier 2 words that students might not know. If you are teaching Grades 6–8 or have strong readers, you may be able to teach multiple animals at the same time (for example, you could teach the Tiger and Camel rules together). It is all about who you are working with and the knowledge they bring to the lesson.

Accuracy and automaticity must also be considered. Students who have been taught the foundational phonics skills required to break down multisyllable words but are not automatic in these skills will require introduction of the animals at a slower pace. They will probably require review and reinforcement of the phonics patterns as you teach the principles of syllabication.

Applying the Steps of Syllabication

1. Identify any affixes and remove them (for now).
2. Identify vowels in the word to determine how many syllables there are. Mark vowels with a small 'v' beneath each one.

m i t t e n
  v   v

3. There are two vowels in *mitten*, therefore there are two syllables.
4. Look at what is between the two vowels. In *mitten* there are two 't's or two consonants and they are not a blend. This means that students will be using the Rabbit rule and dividing between the 2 't's.

mit | ten

150   *Chapter 5: Multisyllable Words*

5. Students decode the two syllables using short vowel sounds because they are both closed syllables. They then blend the two syllables together to read the word *mitten*.

Lessons

Lesson 1: Rabbit (or Walrus)

Note: In these lessons teacher talk is in quotations.

The Rule

When two consonants are between two vowels (and they are not a blend), divide between the consonants (rab-bit).

- Compound words can be included in this list.
- This rule is sometimes called the Walrus rule because *rabbit* has two of the same letters for the double consonant whereas *walrus* demonstrates that the consonants can be the same or different.
- For emergent readers, or those without reading automaticity, scaffold this lesson by starting with words that have the same consonant in the middle (e.g., muf/fin.)
- Remember, consonant blends count as one consonant for this process.

I Do
- "Over the next few weeks, we will be looking at how to break down multisyllable words. When we approach new words, the most important thing that we want to figure out is whether to use a long or short vowel sound for each of the vowels. There are animal names that can help us remember different ways to break down words and decide which vowel sounds to use."
- "The first strategy we will be looking at is the Rabbit rule."
- "For all the animal strategies, the first thing we must do is find out how many syllables are in the word. We do this with written words by identifying the vowels."
- "Let's look at the word *rabbit*. How many vowels are in *rabbit*?"
- Write *rabbit* on the board and demonstrate finding and marking the vowels.

rabbit
 v v

- "There are two vowels in *rabbit*, therefore there are two syllables. In the Rabbit rule, when there are two consonants between vowels, and they are not a blend, you divide between the consonants."

rab | bit
 v   v

- "If you look at the two syllables you will see that they are both closed syllables so the vowels will be short."
- Have students say *rab-bit* aloud or tap their desks for each syllable as they say *rab-bit*.

rab | bit
v   v

- Demonstrate a second time with the word *mitten*, which is shown previously.

We Do

- Have students do a few words with you in their notebooks/binders using the word lists that follow. I strongly recommend you add vocabulary learning into the lesson at this point. The vocabulary you choose will depend on your students. The greater their vocabulary skills, the more complex the words that you will choose. For example, use the word *fossil*.
- Write *fossil* on the board. "What is a fossil?" (Noun: **Preserved** / captured remains of ancient **organisms**/plants and animals.) If you are using rich vocabulary like *preserved* and *organisms* make sure you repeat the concept using Tier 1 vocabulary (included after each word) that all students can understand.
- "Is there another meaning for *fossil*?" (slang for an old person)
- "What would be the opposite of *fossil*?" (a living organism or even a dead one as the fossil just captures its shape and is not the organism itself)
- "Can you think of another word that means *fossil*?" (e.g., specimen, relic, skeleton, trace, impression, deposit)
- "Turn to your partner and see if you can come up with a sentence or two that uses the word *fossil*. Can you create a sentence that refers to the rock **and** an old person?" This is oral work and there is no writing during the generation of sentences.

Note: This type of word exploration supports vocabulary learning and retention. You do not need to do this type of work in this lesson, but it maximizes your teaching time.

- Have students write the word *fossil* in their notebooks/binders.
- Model finding the vowels and have them do the same in their notebooks.

fossil
v   v

"If there are two consonants between the two vowels, and they are not a blend, where would you divide the word?" Have students draw a line between the two s's.

fos | sil
v   v

- "If you look at the two syllables you will see that they are both closed syllables so the vowels will be short."
- Have students say *fos-sil* aloud or tap their desks for each syllable as they say *fos-sil*.
- Under the word, have students write one or two of the sentences they made with their partner.
- Repeat with a word that has two different consonants in the middle (e.g., rustic) and model a word with a blend (e.g., bathtub). Where appropriate, for each concept, work on vocabulary meaning at the same time.

- Write a selection of words on the board and have students segment the words in their notebooks/binders and check all together.

Note: You can see that there is a range of words in the lists below. If your students have low vocabulary skills, use words like *muffin*, *upset*, and *bathtub*. If they have high vocabulary skills, or you would like to push vocabulary in this lesson, use words like *griffin*, *nutmeg*, and *acquit*. Before you reject a word for being too simple, consider multiple meanings and how easy it will be for your students to come up with synonyms and antonyms.

English Language Learners: Use Tier 1 words (e.g., *rabbit, napkin, bathtub*) and include a visual of the word to support understanding and retention.

You Do
- Project a list of Rabbit words on the board and have students break them into syllables.
- Project a list of Rabbit words on the board and have them choose 5 words to break into syllables and then write out the meanings and a sentence.
- Have students generate as many Rabbit words as they can.

Rabbit Word List

Double Consonant		Two Different Consonants		Words with Blends and Digraphs	
address	griffin	batman	picnic	abstract	distress
bonnet	grommet	bedrock	public	acquit	fishnet
cannot	mitten	cactus	rustic	anklet	flipflop
classic	muffin	candid	seldom	backpack	impress
fossil	possum	combat	submit	basket	jackpot
happen	rabbit	fabric	sunset	bathtub	kindred
hiccup	sudden	goblin	tablet	blacktop	muskrat
glutton	tennis	himself	tonsil	complex	pilgrim
goddess	traffic	hundred	trodden	culprit	plankton
gossip	trellis	inlet	uphill	dandruff	pumpkin
		magnet	upset	dishpan	trashcan
		napkin	upshot	inflict	untwist
		nutmeg	velvet		
			victim		

Lesson 2: Tiger

The Rule
- Both Tiger and Camel address the pattern of one consonant between two vowels. When one consonant comes between two vowels, divide after the first vowel, creating an open syllable for the first syllable.
- Approximately 75 percent of words with one consonant between two vowels will be divided this way, so encourage students to try the Tiger rule before the Camel rule (literacylearn.com).
- Remember, consonant blends count as one consonant for this process.

I Do
- "Our second rule for how to break down multisyllable words is the Tiger rule. Remember that as we approach new words, the most important thing we want to figure out is whether to use the long or short vowel sound for each of the vowels."
- "For all the animal strategies, the first thing we must do is find out how many syllables are in the word. We do this with written words by identifying the vowels."
- "Let's look at the word *tiger*. How many vowels are in *tiger*?"
- Write *tiger* on the board and demonstrate finding and marking the vowels.

tiger
v v

- "There are two vowels in *tiger*, therefore there are two syllables. In the Tiger rule, when there is one consonant between vowels you divide after the first vowel. Model this on the board."

ti | ger
v   v

- "This makes the first syllable an open syllable and the second syllable ends with vowel-r and is closed."
- Have students say *ti-ger* aloud or tap their desks for each syllable as they say *ti-ger*.
- Demonstrate a second time with the word *music*.

We Do
- Have students write, mark, and read several Tiger words with you in their notebooks/binders using the following word list.
- Again, add vocabulary learning into the lesson at this point. The vocabulary you choose will depend on your students. The greater their vocabulary skills, the more complex the words that you will choose. For example, use the word *even*, which seems like a simple word but from a vocabulary standpoint is quite complex. **The aim of the vocabulary exploration is to explore and discover** — not teach a complex lesson on the meaning of *even*. Play with the words!
- Write *even* on the board. "What does *even* mean?" (equal, balanced)
- "Is there another meaning for *even*?" (level, smooth). "It can also be used as an adverb to mean 'Can you believe it?' as in 'This burger is **even** bigger than the one I ate yesterday.'"
- "Can you think of another word that means *even*?" (same, tied) OR (level, smooth, flat, unwrinkled) OR (adverb: surprisingly, unexpectedly)
- "What would be the opposite of even?" (unfair, unlike, diverse; rough, warped, wrinkled) OR (adverb: expected)
- "*Even* is an interesting word because it can 'even' be used as an action word (verb). For example, 'You need to even (level off) the batter before you bake the cake.'"
- "Turn to your partner and see if you can come up with sentences that include the word *even* using several of the meanings we just explored. There is no writing at this point, just creating sentences verbally."

This type of word exploration supports vocabulary learning and retention. You do not need to do this type of work in this lesson but it maximizes your teaching time.

- Have students write the word *even* in their notebooks/binders.
- Model finding the vowels and have them do the same in their notebooks.

even
v v

- "If there is one consonant between the two vowels, where would you divide the word?" Have students draw a line after the first 'e.'

e | ven
v   v

- "If you look at the two syllables you will see that the first syllable is an open syllable so the vowel is long. The second syllable is a closed syllable, so the vowel is short." **This is a great word to model as it demonstrates that just one vowel can be a syllable.**
- Have students say *e-ven* aloud or tap their desks for each syllable as they say *e-ven*.
- Students can write one or more of their sentences in their notebooks/binders.
- Repeat with a few more words that have one vowel between two consonants (e.g., tiny – this is a great choice as it demonstrates when 'y' acts as a vowel it says long 'e'). If appropriate, for each concept, work on vocabulary meaning at the same time.
- Write a selection of words on the board and have students segment the words and check all together.

Note: You can see that there is a range of words in the following lists. If your students have low vocabulary skills you can use words like *over, pony*, and *Friday*. If they have high vocabulary skills or you would like to push vocabulary in this lesson, you can use words like *apex, meter*, and *totem*.

English Language Learners: Use Tier 1 words (tiger, pony, ruler) and include a visual of the word to support understanding and retention.

You Do   There is a word sort for Tiger/Camel words after the Camel lesson.
- Project a list of Tiger words on the board and have students break them into syllables.
- Project a second list of Tiger words on the board and have them choose 5 words, break them into syllables, and then write out the meanings.
- Have students generate as many Tiger words as they can.

Tiger Word List

Tier 1 Words		Tier 2 Words	
agent	moment	apex	omit
bacon	motel	basis	pagan
basic	music	biped	propel
began	over	bonus	raven
broken	poker	cement	recent
duplex	polo	climax	recite
even	pony	crisis	relent
event	private	defend	report
ever	recess	elect	rival
evil	report	focus	rodent
fever	ruler	futon	sinus
Friday	secret	haven	totem
gravy	shady	human	tripod
item	silent	humid	truly
ivy	spider	iris	unit
label	student	labor/labour	vacant
lazy	stupid	lotus	vital
meter	tiny	modal	
minus	tulip	omen	

Lesson 3: Camel

The Rule

- When one consonant comes between two vowels, try the Tiger rule first.
- If the Tiger rule does not make sense, divide after the second vowel to create a closed syllable for the first syllable.
- Approximately 25 percent of words will be divided this way.
- Remember, consonant blends count as one consonant for this process.

I Do

- Introduce the Camel rule, reminding students that when there is one consonant between two vowels, they should start with the Tiger rule since most words will use that pattern. If the Tiger rule does not work, then they should try the Camel rule. The first syllable will be closed so the vowel is short (cam-el).
- Use the teaching pattern of the previous lessons.
- Find and mark the vowels:

camel
v   v

- Divide after the consonant:

cam | el
v   v

- Note that the first syllable is closed. Say the word while tapping the syllables.
- Repeat with another word.

We Do
1. Work together to segment 2–3 more words.
2. Look at the vocabulary of the word before segmenting, using the same prompts as above:
    a. The meaning or meanings of the word.
    b. Words that have a similar meaning (synonyms).
    c. Words that have an opposite meaning (antonyms).
    d. Have students work in groups of 2–3 to verbally create sentences that use this word.
3. Have students write the words and several of their sentences in their notebooks/binders.

You Do
- **Word Sort:** Have students segment and sort Tiger and Camel words. You can do this by projecting them onto your board using a document camera or by using the attached worksheets. **Worksheet A** uses Tier 1 words and **Worksheet B** uses Tier 2 words.
- The word lists below are sorted by difficulty in meaning, not spelling.
- **Scaffolding:** Scaffold the word lists in the worksheet by having students sort 6 or 8 words of their choice.
- Students with complex needs who are fortunate to work with an educational assistant can do this work in a variety of settings. While walking, using a stationary bike, or doodling/drawing, the adult can work on segmenting verbally as well as vocabulary meaning (e.g., multiple meanings, antonyms, synonyms).

Camel Word List

Tier 1 Words		Tier 2 Words	
boxer	prison	avid	novel
cabin	proper	banish	panic
camel	punish	cavern	pedal
closet	radish	chapel	petal
comic	rapid	clinic	planet
copy	river	comet	profit
dragon	salad	credit	quiver
ever	second	critic	rabid
honest	seven	frigid	ravel
lemon	solid	lavish	ravish
limit	study	legend	rebel
magic	sturdy	level	relish
melon	travel	linen	timid
menu	visit	model	tonic
metal			topic

Lesson 4: Lion

The Rule

When two vowels are together and they are not a vowel team, divide between the two vowels.

I Do
- Introduce the Lion rule, reminding students that when there are no consonants between two vowels, they must check that the two vowels are not a vowel team. This may require review of vowel teams. To support this lesson and students who are still learning vowel teams, you can post a list of vowel teams in your classroom (see example below).
- When dividing between two vowels, the first syllable will be open, so the vowel is long (li-on).
- Demonstrate this rule following the teaching pattern used in the lessons above.
- Find and mark the vowels:

    lion
    v v

- Divide between the vowels:

    li | on
    v   v

- Note that the first syllable is open. Say the word while tapping the syllables.
- Repeat with another word.

We Do
1. Work together to segment 2–3 more words.
2. Look at the vocabulary of the word before segmenting using the same prompts as above:
    a. The meaning or meanings of the word.
    b. Words that have a similar meaning (synonyms).
    c. Words that have an opposite meaning (antonyms).
    d. Have students work in groups of 2–3 to verbally create sentences that use this word.
3. Have students write the words and several of their sentences in their notebooks/binders.

You Do Write a selection of words on the board that have vowel teams (see lists starting on the next page) and Lion rule words. Ask students to sort words by vowel team and Lion words. Ask students to break all words into syllables.

Common Vowel Teams Chart

"a" Sound	"e" Sound	"i" Sound	"o" Sound	"u" Sound	Diphthongs
ai - main	ea - seat	ie - tie	oa - boat	ew - pew	oi - boil
ay - tray	ee - peel	igh - sigh	oe - toe	ue - due	oy - toy
ey - obey	ei - receive			eu - feud	ou - soup, mouth
eigh - sleigh	ie - thief				ow - town
ei - vein	ey - key				au - August
					aw - bawl
					oo - look, moon

Lion Word List		
Tier 1: Two Syllables	**Tier 2: Two Syllables**	**Three Syllables**
create	Buick	influence
dial	chaos	iodine
diet	client	museum
duet	coerce	pioneer
duo	fluent	rodeo
fuel	fluid	Romeo
giant	ion	violent
idea	neon	violet
lion	oasis	violin
meow	riot	
poem	scion	
poet	stoic	
quiet	trial	
ruin	truant	
science		
triumph		
	With affixes	
	rearm	
	react	

Lesson 5: Turtle

Review the Consonant+le rule on page 137 before this lesson.

The Rule

- Consonant+le always occurs at the END of words.
- Consonant+le only occurs in multisyllabic words.
- The 'le' plus the consonant before it forms a syllable. Even though the 'e' is silent, it is the vowel of the consonant.
- The -le will make the /əl/ sound, which sounds like /ŭl/ (it includes a schwa sound).

Lessons 159

I Do
- Teach or review the Consonant-le rule.
- Introduce the Turtle rule, reminding students that when there is an 'le' at the end of a multisyllable word, the 'le' and the consonant before it forms a syllable (tur-tle). The 'e' is silent but is the vowel in the consonant.
- Model the syllabication of Turtle words using the teaching pattern of the lessons above.
- Find and underline the 'le':

turt<u>le</u>

- Add the consonant before the 'le' to form the syllable and divide the word:

tur | t<u>le</u>

- The first syllable may be open or closed depending on the word. 'tur' in *turtle* is a closed syllable whereas the 'bug' in *bugle* is open, bu-gle. Many students read this as 'buggle' because they do not understand the consonant-le rule. Say the word while tapping the syllables.
- Repeat with another word.

We Do
- Work together to segment 2 or 3 additional words.
- Look at the vocabulary of the word before segmenting using the same prompts as above:
  - The meaning or meanings of the word.
  - Words that have a similar meaning (synonyms).
  - Words that have an opposite meaning (antonyms).
  - Have students work in groups of 2 or 3 to verbally create sentences that use this word.
- Have students write the words and several of their sentences in their notebooks/binders.

You Do Post a collection of Turtle words on the board and have students segment them in their notebook/binder.

Lesson 6: Multisyllable Words with Affixes

See Consonant-le rule (page 137) for the word list you can use here.

When decoding multisyllable words, it is helpful for students to begin by identifying affixes, when applicable. Review identifying affixes and employ the word list for Consonant-le (page 140). In this example, we will identify affixes using the word *reconstructed*.

<u>re</u>construct<u>ed</u>

Once the affixes have been identified, students can apply syllabication to break the word into syllables. First, they identify the vowels. There are two vowels in *construct* so there are two syllables.

<u>re</u>constructe<u>d</u>
v   v

The next step is to look at what is between the two vowels: nstr. 'Str' is a blend so it must stay together which means the division is between two consonants (one is a blend). This is the Rabbit rule.

<u>re</u> con | struct <u>ed</u>

There are two closed syllables so the vowels are short.

Once the two syllables have been sounded out, the student puts them together to sound out the word: *construct*. From our morphology lessons we know that 'struct' is to build and 'con' is together, so the word *construct* means to put together to build something.

Now include the affixes when decoding: *reconstructed*. The student applies the knowledge that *re-* means again and *-ed* means it is in the past, so the meaning of the word is that someone built something again before today.

<u>re</u>con<u>struct</u><u>ed</u>

I Do:
- Teach or review the lesson on affixes and bases first (page 61).
- Following the example above, show students that when decoding multisyllable words it is helpful to identify prefixes and suffixes before breaking the word into syllables.
- Identify the affixes by underlining or circling them.

<u>mis</u>label<u>ed</u>

- Once the affixes have been identified and removed, identify the vowels.

<u>mis</u>label<u>ed</u>
　　v　v

- Identify the animal pattern, which for *label* would be the Tiger rule. Divide into syllables and decode the word.

<u>mis</u> | la | bel | <u>ed</u>
　　　　v　　v

- Read the word, including the affixes.

<u>mis</u> | la | bel | <u>ed</u>
　　　　v　　v

- Review the meaning of the word.

We Do
- Continue to model multisyllable words with affixes to ensure students have a firm understanding of the steps.
- Have students follow along by writing them in their notebooks/binders.
- Ask if there are volunteers who would like to come up to the board and model the process with a multisyllable word.

You Do
- Provide students with a list of multisyllable words to work with independently. Be prepared to explore and play with words.
- **Worksheet:** Multisyllable Words with Affixes

Word List: Multisyllable Words with Affixes		
antivirus	misplaced	replaying
disabled	misprinting	rethinking
disagreeable	misunderstanding	rewriting
disembark	misunderstood	scoreless
impatiently	mainly	semicircles
impressive	midyears	semicolon
display	painless	softness
healthy	payment	unclear
incompletely	planted	undrinkable
independently	preheating	unteachable
ineffective	prepay	untrusting
ingrained	reconstruct	unsupportive
irregular	reorganized	weakness
misadventures	repeated	
misbehaving		

Lesson 7: Schwa in Multisyllable Words

This is a good place to revisit schwa (see Chapter 4, Lesson 2), as schwa is found in the unaccented syllables of multisyllable words.

Also known as double agents, these letters make decoding challenging. Helping students understand and identify these letters will strengthen decoding multisyllable words.

The Rule

This rule is a generalization and not always true. When breaking down multisyllable words, there is one syllable that is accented and then one or more syllables that are unaccented. For example, in the word *wagon* more stress is placed on the syllable 'wag' than 'on.' In *wagon*, the 'o' in the second syllable becomes a schwa and sounds more like 'un' - /wagun/.

I Do
- Reteach or review the concept of schwa (page 113).
- Using multisyllable words, show students examples of where schwa is present. Examples might include wag**on**, **be**low, ang**el**.

We Do
- Write or project words from the schwa word list (page 116) on the board. Read as a class and identify where schwa is present and how this impacts decoding multisyllable words.
- Note how often schwa shows up in the second syllable of two-syllable words.

Camel/Tiger Worksheet A

Name: _____

For each of the words below, **sort them** into Camel and Tiger words. Once sorted, identify the vowels and show where the word is divided into syllables.

Word Bank			
boxer	music	magic	private
student	menu	proper	comic
recess	moment	ruler	visit
silent	dragon	seven	report

Ti-ger	Cam-el

Antonyms (opposite):

Choose 2 of the words above and write one or two antonyms (opposite meaning) for each word.

1. _____ : _____
2. _____ : _____

Synonyms (the same):

Choose 2 of the words above and write one or two synonyms (same meaning) for each word.

1. _____ : _____
2. _____ : _____

Multiple Meanings

Can you find words in the list above that have multiple meanings? What are they?

_____ : _____
_____ : _____

Camel/Tiger Worksheet B

Name: _____

For each of the words below, **sort them** into Camel and Tiger words. Once sorted, identify the vowels and show where the word is divided into syllables.

Word Bank			
avid	sinus	propel	rabid
critic	modal	relent	tonic
novel	apex	planet	quiver
haven	ravel	elect	cavern

Ti-ger	**Cam-el**

Antonyms:

Choose 2 of the words above and write one or two antonyms (opposite meaning) for each word.

1. _____ : _____
2. _____ : _____

Synonyms

Choose 2 of the words above and write one or two synonyms (the same meaning) for each word.

1. _____ : _____
2. _____ : _____

Multiple Meanings

Find 2 words in the list above that have multiple meanings. What are they?

1. _____ : _____
2. _____ : _____

Camel/Tiger Worksheet B (cont'd)

Adding Affixes		
Choose 6 of the words above and add at least one prefix and one suffix to the word. Define your word and use it in a sentence.		
Word	**Meaning**	**Sentence**
Example: level: releveled	something has been made horizontal again	They releveled the table because the cups were still sliding off and falling on the floor.

Multisyllable Words with Affixes

Name: _____

Choose 7 words from the word bank and write them on the blanks below. Circle each affix and divide the word into syllables.

Word Bank

disagreeable	misunderstood	impatiently	reorganized
rethinking	misprinting	ingrained	unsupportive
independently	semicircles	preheating	incompletely
misadventures	misbehaving	undrinkable	repeated
unteachable	rewriting	ineffective	

(re)|writ|(ing)   _____   _____   _____

_____   _____   _____   _____

For 5 of your words, choose one syllable and write as many words as you can with that syllable.

Rewriting – write: prewrite, writes, writable, rewrite, miswrite, unwritable

1. _____

2. _____

3. _____

4. _____

5. _____

Recommended Resources

Structured Language and Literacy

10 Maxims by G.R. Lyon
Lyon, G.R. (n.d.). *10 Maxims: What we've learned so far about how children learn to read.* Reading Universe Prototype. https://readinguniverse.org/article/explore-teaching-topics/big-picture/ten-maxims-what-weve-learned-so-far-about-how-children-learn-to-read

Reading Rockets
WETA (2024). Reading Rockets: Launching Young Readers. https://www.readingrockets.org

Teaching Reading is Rocket Science
Moats, L.C. Teaching Reading is Rocket Science. *American Educator, Summer 2020.* 44–2.

Screening and Assessments

Academic Screening Tools Chart
National Center on Intensive Intervention (2021). Academic Screening Tools Chart. https://charts.intensiveintervention.org/ascreening

Acadience
Acadience Reading (n.d.). Reading Screening Tools.
Grades K–6: https://acadiencelearning.org/acadience-reading/k-grade6/
Grades 7–8: https://acadiencelearning.org/acadience-reading/acadience-reading-7-8/

AIM Institute: Quick Guide for Reading Assessment
AIM Institute for Learning and Research (2021). Quick Guide for Reading Assessment. Nebraska Department of Education. https://www.education.ne.gov/wp-content/uploads/2022/05/AIM-Quick-Guide-to-Reading-Assessment.pdf

Cubed
Language Dynamics Group (2024). Cubed-3. https://www.languagedynamicsgroup.com/cubed/

DIBELS 8
University of Oregon (n.d.). DIBELS: Dynamic Indicators of Basic Early Literacy Skills. https://dibels.uoregon.edu/materials/dibels

Easy CBM
Behavioral Research and Teaching (n.d.). Easy CBM: Response to Intervention Made Easy. https://www.easycbm.com/

Multi-Tiers System of Support
American Institutes for Research (n.d.). Essential components of MTSS Center on multi-tiered systems of supports. https://mtss4success.essential-components

Reading Rockets Screening and Assessment
Screening and Assessment (n.d.) Reading rockets. Retrieved February 2024, from https://www.readingrockets.org/helping-all-readers/screening-and-assessment

Phonics

Orthographic Mapping Explainer by Lyn Stone
Stone, L. (2019). *Orthographic Mapping Explainer.* YouTube. https://www.youtube.com/watch?v=KIuwKnZqJEQ

Reading Rev
Luna, B. (n.d.). Reading Rev: All Things Literacy! https://readingrev.com/

Spelling Words Well
Fisher, A.R. (2024). Spelling Words Well. https://www.spelling-words-well.com/index.html

This is How We Teach Reading… And It's Working!
Willms, H. & Alberti, G. (2022) *This is How We Teach Reading… And It's Working!* Pembroke Publishers Limited. https://www.pembrokepublishers.com/book.cgi?isbn=9781551383576

Word Game World
Fisher, A.R. (2024). Word-Game-World.com. https://www.word-game-world.com

Wordle (New York Times)
New York Times (2024). Wordle. Edited by Tracy Bennett. https://www.nytimes.com/games/wordle/index.html

Wordle for Kids (Wordly)
Wordly.org (2024). Wordle for Kids. https://wordly.org/wordle-for-kids

Decodable Texts

Decodable Text Generator from Project Read
Project Read (2024). Decodable Stories Generator. https://www.projectread.ai/

GO! Decode TwERL Series
Saunders Book Company (2024). GO! Decode: TwERL Phonics. https://www.saundersbook.ca/series/WSDL5044

The Meg and Greg Book Series
Rae, E. & Rae, R. (n.d.). Meg and Greg Series. Orca Book Publishers. https://www.orcabook.com/Elementary?ShopBy=1615

Orton Gillingham Online Academy
Orton Gillingham Online Academy (n.d.). https://ortongillinghamonlinetutor.com/
Great reading passages can be found in their 'Developing Fluency' package. Newsletter recipients are offered inexpensive pricing several times a year.

Phonics Play Comics
Phonics Play Comics (n.d.). Decodable Comics that follow the teaching sequence of Letters and Sounds. https://phonicsplaycomics.co.uk/comics.html

ReadWorks Decodable Passages
ReadWorks (2020). Decodable Passages by Concept. https://www.readworks.org/teacher-guide/decodables-by-concept.html

UFLI Decodable Passages
UFLI Foundations (2022). Decodable Passages. https://ufli.education.ufl.edu/wp-content/uploads/2023/02/UFLI-Foundations-Decodables-ALL.pdf

West Virginia Phonics Passages
West Virginia Department of Education (n.d.). Phonics Passages. Marshall University. https://www.marshall.edu/juneharless/jhc-programs/early-learning-technical-assistance-center/

Word Connections by Jessica Toste
Toste, J. R., Capin, P., Williams, K. J., Kearns, D. M., & Vaughn, S. (2023). *Word connections: A multisyllabic word reading program, 2nd Ed.* figshare. https://doi.org/10.6084/m9.figshare.c.6259368

Reading Passages: Non Decodable Accessible Text

Everyday Edits: Education World
Education World (2024). Every-Day Edits. https://www.educationworld.com/a_lesson/archives/edit.shtml

High Noon Books
High Noon Books (2024). Academic Therapy Publications. https://highnoonbooks.academictherapy.com/

National Geographic Kids Passage Reading
National Geographic Kids (n.d.). Primary Resources: Passage Reading. https://www.natgeokids.com/uk/teacher-category/primary-resources/

Uncovering the Logic of English by Denise Eide
Logic of English (2024). Free Resources Based on the Science of Reading. https://resources.logicofenglish.com/

Word Connections by Jessica Toste
Toste, J. (n.d.). Word Connections. https://www.jessicatoste.com
Toste and her team have created this multisyllabic word reading program designed for older students. It is full of short reading passages and word lists.

Audiobooks

Audible
Audible, Inc. (2024). *(available paid and free)* Make Reading Richer with Audio. https://audible.ca or https://audible.com

CalibreAudio
CalibreAudio (2024). *(Free for students who struggle with text)* Overseas Members. https://www.calibreaudio.org.uk/services/overseas

Epic Books
Epic Books (n.d.). *(paid)* Over 40 000 digital books. https://www.getepic.com

LibriVox
LibriVox (n.d.). *(free)* Free public domain audio books. https://librivox.org/
You and your students can even sign up to be a volunteer reader.

Public Libraries
(free) Public libraries provide access to audio books online. Many libraries use Hoopla and Libby (OverDrive app) in Canada and the United States, and some libraries offer both. Students will require a library card and this is an excellent reason to encourage students and families to sign up for access to their local library.
Hoopla: https://www.hoopladigital.com/browse/audiobook
Libby: https://libbyapp.com/interview/welcome#doYouHaveACard

SORA
SORA (n.d.). *(free with school account)* https://soraapp.com/
SORA is available through schools. If your school provides access to SORA, students will be able to access it at home.

Spotify
Spotify (2024). *(paid and free)* Get lost in great stories. https://spotify.com/ca-en/audiobooks/

Storynory
Storynory (n.d.). *(free)* Fairy tales, myths and fables. https://www.storynory.com/

Vocabulary

Academic Word List
EAP Foundation (2024). The Academic Word List (AWL). https://www.eapfoundation.com/vocab/academic/awllists/

Academic Word List by Frequency
EAP Foundation (2024). New General Word List (NGSL). https://www.eapfoundation.com/vocab/general/ngsl/

Connections (New York Times)
New York Times (n.d.). Connections. Edited by Wyna Liu. https://www.nytimes.com/games/connections

Connections for Kids
Connections Game (2023). Connections Game NYT for Kids. Edited by Evan Little. https://connectionsgame.org/blog/connections-game-nyt-for-kids-play-online-free/

Word of the Day: Dictionary.com
Dictionary.com (2024). Word of the Day. https://www.dictionary.com/

Morphology

The Morphology Project
The Grammar Project (n.d.). The Morphology Project. https://thesyntaxproject2022.squarespace.com/the-morphology-project

Syntax Matters by William Van Cleave
Van Cleave, W (2020). *Syntax Matters: The Link Between Sentence Writing and Sentence Comprehending*. https://www.youtube.com/watch?v=0GuAXma77FI

The William Van Cleave Wakelet, created by Pam Kastner
Kastner, P (2024). The William Van Cleave Wakelet. https://wakelet.com/wake/XuIDNfx7OXoxLImeFyalj

The William Van Cleave Website
W.V.C.ED (2019). The William Van Cleave website. https://www.wvced.com/

Fluency

The Dyslexia Classroom
Harrison, C. (2024). The Dyslexia Classroom: Where Learning Takes Flight. https://www.thedyslexiaclassroom.com

Microsoft Reading Progress for Fluency
Microsoft Teams for Education (2024). Microsoft Reading Progress. https://support.microsoft.com/en-us/topic/getting-started-with-reading-progress-in-teams-7617c11c-d685-4cb7-8b75-3917b297c407

Six Minute Solutions
Adams, G.N. & Brown, S.M. (n.d.) The Six-Minute Solution: A Reading Fluency Program. https://www.voyagersopris.com/docs/default-source/literacy/six-minute-solution/six-minute-overview.pdf

This Reading Mama
Spence, B. (2024). This Reading Mama. https://thisreadingmama.com

Trauma

Trauma and Reading with Dr. Steven Dykstra
Dykstra, Dr. S. "Trauma and Reading". Melissa & Lori Love Literacy. Podcast audio, April 1, 2022. https://podcasts.apple.com/us/podcast/ep-100-traumaand-reading-with-dr-steven-dykstra/id1463219123?i=1000555942998

References

Allison, D. J. (2023, December 20). Children's socialization and returning to social norms post COVID. Fraser Institute. https://www.fraserinstitute.org/article/reading-and-math-scores-plummet-across-canada-after-covid-school-closures

Archer, A. L., & Hughes, C.A. (2011). *Explicit instruction: Effective and efficient teaching*. The Gilford Press.

Beck, I. L., McKeown, M. G., & Kucan K. (2013). https://www.speld.org.au/files/blog/robust_vocab_instruction_beck_mckeown_kucan_2.pdf

Bowers, P. N. (2007). *Teaching how the written word works*. WordWorks. Literacy Centre.

Bowers, P. N., & Kirby, J. R. (2010). Effects of morphological instruction on vocabulary acquisition. *Read Writ* 23, 515–537 (2010). https://doi.org/10.1007/s11145-009-9172-z

Bowman, A. (2023, June 29). Children's socialization and returning to social norms post COVID. Mayo Clinic Press. https://mcpress.mayoclinic.org/parenting/childrens-socialization-and-social-skills-post-covid/

Centre for Education Policy Research at Harvard University (2023, May 11). New research finds that pandemic learning loss impacted whole communities, regardless of student race or income. Retrieved Aug 24 from https://cepr.harvard.edu/news/new-research-finds-pandemic-learning-loss-impacted-whole-communities-regardless-student

Council of Ministers of Education, Canada. (2023). Measuring up: Canadian results of the OECD PISA 2022 Study. Retrieved Aug 24 from https://www.cmec.ca/Publications/Lists/Publications/Attachments/438/PISA-2022_Canadian_Report_EN.pdf

Coxhead, A. (n.d.). The academic word list (AWL). EAP Foundation.com. https://www.eapfoundation.com/vocab/academic/awllists/

Cunningham, A. E., & Stanovich, K. E. (1997). Early reading acquisition and its relation to reading experience and ability 10 years later. Developmental Psychology, 33, 6, 934-945.

Cunningham, A. E., & Stanovich, K. E. (1998). What reading does to the mind. American Federation of Teachers.

Dehaene, S. (2009). *Reading in the brain: The new science of how we read.* Penguin Books.

Dehaene, S. (2021). *How we learn to read.* Penguin Books.

Di Salvo, F. (2024, March 9). Science root words. https://fabiodisalvo.com/2022/05/22/sciencAk3PAlIlOJEpr-SK7o7shPf-ZLtRhmQ-ZuQwTl8rbE0SsJDt4 e-root-words/?fbclid=IwAR2r9UEjD0

Doughty, C. (2019, June 17). Where does the phrase pull up your socks come from & what's its meaning? https://socksnob.co.uk/the-phrase-pull-up-your-socks/

Drysdale, W. (Ed.). (1887). *Proverbs from Plymouth pulpit: Selected from the writings and sayings of Henry Ward Beecher.* D. Appleton and Company. This work appears in the public domain of the United States.

Dubosarsky, U. (2009). *The word snoop: A wild and witty tour of the English language!* Dial Books.

Duke, N. K., & Cartwright, K. B. (2021). The science of reading progresses: Communicating advances beyond the simple view of reading. *Reading Research Quarterly, 56*(S1), S25-S44.

Dykstra, Dr. S. "Trauma and Reading". *Melissa & Lori Love Literacy.* Podcast audio, April 1, 2022. https://podcasts.apple.com/us/podcast/ep-100-trauma-and-reading-with-dr-steven-dykstra/id1463219123?i=1000555942998

Eide, D. (2011). *Uncovering the logic of English.* Pedia Learning Inc.

Ehri, L. C. (2013). Orthographic mapping in the acquisition of sight word reading, spelling memory, and vocabulary learning. *Scientific Studies of Reading, 18*(1), 5–21. https://doi-org.ezproxy.viu.ca/10.1080/10888438.2013.819356

Ethier, S. (2017, November 14). Why Canadian spelling is different. Retrieved from https://www.noslangues-ourlanguages.gc.ca/en/blogue-blog/canadian-spelling-eng

Frank, M. (2018, March). Morpheme matrices: Sequential or standalone lessons for assembling common prefixes, Latin roots, Greek forms, and suffixes. https://atlasabe.org/wp-content/uploads/2019/04/Morpheme_Matrices-rev072120.pdf?fbclid=IwAR2UTx-0IlN_7PmfHeYWb-kfxoAKJMf0YqTBeTPKmJhy-8OP4lDuRGH9_ls&mibextid=Zxz2cZ

Ginseng English. (n.d.). Silent k words. Retrieved from https://ginsengenglish.com/

Gough, P., & Tunmer, W. (1986). Decoding, reading, and reading disability. *Remedial and Special Education, 7,* 6-10.

Harrison, C. (n.d.) The dyslexia classroom. Retrieved from https://www.thedyslexiaclassroom.com/

Kilpatrick, D. A. (2016). *Equipped for reading success.* Casey & Kirsch Consulting.

Learn That Foundation. Root words and prefixes: Quick reference. https://www.learnthat.org/pages/view/roots.html?fbclid=IwAR1HDdy9Zj21YLByaRF88DAPXiP9jgwIRGFfajLRyiy-3NXVloY326-CFUQ#a

Lyon, G.R. (n.d.). *10 Maxims: What we've learned so far about how children learn to read.* Reading Universe Prototype. https://readinguniverse.org/article/explore-teaching-topics/big-picture/ten-maxims-what-weve-learned-so-far-about-how-children-learn-to-read

Manyak, P. C., Baumann, J. F., & Manyak, A. (2018, November/December). Morphological analysis instruction in the elementary grades: Which morphemes to teach and how to teach them. *The Reading Teacher, Vol 72 (3),* 289-300.

Mather, N., Wendling, B. L., & Roberts, R. (2009). *Writing assessment and instruction for students with learning disabilities, 2nd Ed.* Jossey-Bass.

McKeown, M. G. (2019, October 10). Effective vocabulary instruction fosters knowing words, using words, and understanding how words work. *Language, Speech & Hearing Services in Schools,* Vol 50 (4), 466-476. https://DOI:10.1044/2019_LSHSS-VOIA-18-0126

Moats, L. C. (2005). How spelling supports reading. *American Educator, Winter 2005/06,* 12-43.

Moats, L. C. (2019, July). Teaching spelling: An opportunity to unveil the logic of language. *Perspectives on Language and Literacy,* Vol 44 (3), 17-20.

Moats, L. C. (2020). *Speech to print: Language essentials for teachers (3rd Edition).* Brookes Publishing.

Moats, L. C., & Tolman, C. A. (2019). LETRS, *3rd Ed.* Voyager Sopris Learning.

Nagy, W., Berninger, V. W., & Abbott, R. D. (2006). Contributions of morphology beyond phonology to literacy outcomes of upper elementary and middle-school students. *Journal of Educational Psychology,* 98(1), 134–147. https://doi.org/10.1037/0022-0663.98.1.134

NIH. (2000). National reading panel. Retrieved December 2023, from https://www.nichd.nih.gov/research/supported/

Pedagogy Non Grata (n.d.). Evidence-based education. https://www.teachingbyscience.com/

Programme for International Student Assessment (PISA). https://www.oecd.org/en/about/programmes/pisa.html

Right to Read (2022). Public inquiry into human rights issues affecting students with reading disabilities. Ontario Human Rights Commission.

Rose, J. (2006, March). *Independent review of the teaching of early reading: Final report.* Department of Education & Skills, 0201-2006DOC-EN. https://dera.ioe.ac.uk/5551/2/report.pdf

Rowe, K., Devine, M., Knight, F., Louden, B., Lovat, T., Meyer, Y., Ramsey, G., Rice, A., Scalfino, L., & Smith, K. (2005, December). *Teaching reading: National inquiry into the teaching of literacy.* Australian Government Department of Education, Training and Science.

Rymanowicz, K. (2017, April 3). Children and empathy: Reading to learn empathy. Retrieved April 15, 2022, from https://www.canr.msu.edu/news/children_and_empathy_reading_to_learn_empathy

Shanahan, T. (2018, May 19). Comprehension skills or strategies: Is there a difference and does it matter? Shanahan on Literacy. https://www.shanahanonliteracy.com/blog/comprehension-skills-or-strategies-is-there-a-difference-and-does-it-matter

Spence, B. (n.d.) This reading mama. Retrieved from https://thisreadingmama.com/

St. Martin, K., Vaughn, S., Troia, G., Fien, H., & Coyne, M. (2023). Intensifying literacy instruction: Essential practices, Version 2.0. MiMTSS Technical Assistance Center, Michigan Department of Education.

Stahl, S., & Nagy, W. (2006). *Teaching word meanings.* Lawrence Erlbaum.

Stone, L. (2018, Winter) Activities for practicing spelling – Toxic to helpful. *LAD Bulletin,* Vol 50 (2). https://www.scribd.com/document/669641363/Activities-for-Practising-Spelling-Toxic-to-Helpful-Lyn-Stone

Vollmer, J. (2011, November 8). *The blueberry story: The teacher gives the businessman a lesson.* University of Nebraska-Lincoln. https://newsroom.unl.edu/announce/csmce/755/3329

Vyduna-Haskins, G. (n.d.). The spel-lang tree: A word study program. https://sites.google.com/view/spel-langtree/home

White, T. G., Sowell, G., & Yanagihara, A. (1989, January). Teaching elementary students to use word part clues. *The Reading Teacher, Vol 42 (4)*, pp. 302-308. https://www.jstor.org/stable/20200115

Willms, H., & Alberti, C. (2022). *This is how we teach reading… and it's working.* Pembroke Publishers.

Index

accuracy, 19, 21, 148, 150
active, self-regulatory processes, 13–14
affixes
    bases and, 61, 66–67
    described, 57–58, 59
    Latin, 59–61
    lessons, 66–67
    multisyllable words with, 61, 160–162, 166
    review, 84
    sorting, 76
    spelling, 64
    word sort, 85–86
    worksheet, 83
'ai' and 'ay' vowel teams, 122–123
anchor charts, 40–41
animal patterns
    camel, 149, 156–157, 163–165
    described, 149–150
    lion, 149, 158–159
    rabbit, 149, 151–153
    tiger, 149, 153–156, 163–165
    turtle, 149, 159–160
    walrus, 151–153
antonyms
    described, 32
    spelling challenge, 104
    word bank, 41
    worksheet, 54
'ar' vowel-r, 128–129
assessment
    classroom intervention materials, 21–22
    described, 16
    English Language Learners (ELLs), 22–23
    intervention, 20–21
    multi-tiered system of supports (MTSS), 17–18
    oral reading fluency, 18–19
    parents reading to students, 23–24
    phonemic awareness, 19
    phonics and word reading assessments, 19
    purpose, 18
    spelling and assessments, 19
    timeline, 20
assimilated prefixes, 58
audiobooks, 23
automaticity, 21, 150
'aw' and 'au' vowel teams, "126

balanced literacy, 15
baseline, 20
bases
    activities, 75–76
    affixes and, 61, 66–67
    bound, 57, 58, 67
    described, 57, 58
    free, 57, 58, 66–67
    Latin, 60–61
    lessons, 66–67
    review, 84
    word sort, 85–86
    worksheet, 82
basic interpersonal communication skills (BICS), 29–30
BINGO card games, 42, 107–108
blends, 148
bound base, 57, 58, 67
"breaking the code", 14
bt (silent letter), 118–121
bulletin boards, 77

'c' (hard and soft)
    lesson, 129–131
    rule, 130
    word lists, 131–132
    worksheets, 145–146
'ch' digraphs, 140–141
chapter summary, 26
class dictionary, 108–109
class lists, 79
closed syllables, 110–113, 148
cognitive academic language proficiency (CALP), 29–30
complex behaviours, 11
complex consonants
    lesson, 135–137
    pattern rule, 135–136
    rule, 136–137
    word list, 137
complex lists, 98
components of reading instruction
    comprehension, 13, 15
    described, 13–14
    fluency, 13, 15
    phonemic awareness, 13, 14
    phonics, 13, 14
    phonological awareness, 13, 14
    vocabulary, 13, 15
comprehension, 13, 15, 96
connecting vowel letters, 63–64
Connections, 39–40
connector words, 31, 63
consonant-le
    exceptions, 138–139
    lesson, 137–139
    reading, 138
    rule, 137, 139
    spelling, 138
    syllable rule, 148
    word lists, 140
    worksheet, 144
consonant-vowel-consonant (CVC) words, 8
context, 31

decodable texts, 22
decoding, 14, 94–95, 148–149
derivational suffixes, 58
'dge' complex consonants, 135–137
diacritic, 117
diagnostic assessments, 17
dictation, 100, 103
dictionary, 108–109
digraphs
    'ch', 140–141
    described, 98, 118
    'ph', 141
    review, 148

176   *Index*

spelling, 118–121
diphthongs
   chart, 159
   described, 121
   'oi' and 'oy', 127
   'ou', 126–127
   'ow' and 'ou', 127–128
doubling rule
   lesson, 67–68
   worksheet, 74

editing, 105
'ee' and 'ea' vowel teams, 124–125
encoding, 14, 94–95
English Language Learners (ELLs), 22–23
'er' vowel-r, 128–129
error types, 19
etymology, 16, 119
Explain It to Me!, 40
expressive vocabulary, 27

50/50 spelling game, 105–106
flashcards, 77–79
floss rule, 98
fluency
   apps, 22
   described, 13, 15
   oral reading, 18–19
   spelling, 96
free base, 57, 58, 66–67
functional vocabulary
   described, 31
   examples, 31–32

'g' (hard and soft)
   lesson, 133–134
   rule, 133
   word list, 135
gh (silent letter), 118–121
gn (silent letter), 118–121
graphemes
   described, 14, 95, 101
   spelling, 101–103, 117
Greek combining forms
   activity, 75–76
   described, 61–63
   worksheet, 82
Greek idioms
   teaching, 43–46
   worksheet, 55
Greek words
   'ch' digraph, 140–141
   'ph' digraph, 141

silent letters, 142
'y' sounds, 141–142

head words, 30
heteronyms
   described, 32
   quirky, 47, 50–51
   working with, 47
   worksheet, 48–49
homographs
   described, 32
   worksheet, 54
homonyms, 32
homophones
   bulletin board, 42
   described, 32
   silent letters and, 118
   worksheet, 52–53, 54

I Do / We Do / You Do instruction model, 101
idioms
   described, 33
   examples, 45–46
   Greek, 43–46, 55
'igh' trigraph, 126
inflexed suffixes, 58
intervention
   classroom materials, 21–22
   described, 20–21
'ir' vowel-r, 128–129
Is It Spelled Correctly?, 106–107
It's Up to You!, 107

kn (silent letter), 118–121

Learning Support Teacher, 21

marking spelling, 100–101
matrices
   creating words with, 76
   student-built, 76
   worksheets, 87–92
mb (silent letter), 118–121
morpheme
   class lists, 79
   described, 56
   oral manipulation, 77
   word sorts, 79–80
morphological awareness, 56
morphology
   activities, 75–80

connecting vowel letters, 63–64
curriculum and, 65
described, 16, 56
flashcards, 77–79
Greek combining forms, 61–63
Latin-derived words, 57–61
lessons, 66–74
practices, 64–65
purpose, 56
stressed syllables, 63
vocabulary, 32–33
worksheets, 81–92
multisyllable words
   affixes, 61, 160–162, 166
   animal patterns, 149–150
   blends, 148
   decoding, 148–149
   described, 147
   digraphs, 148
   foundational knowledge, 148–149
   lessons, 151–162
   morphology, 56
   open and closed syllables, 110
   passage reading, 34
   rules, 147–148
   schwa in, 162
   syllabication, 149, 150–151
   vowel teams, 121
   vowel-y ending, 70
   word reading, 110–111
   worksheets, 163–166
multi-tiered system of supports (MTSS), 17–18

'oa' and 'ow' vowel teams, 123–124
'oi' and 'oy' diphthongs, 127
'oo' vowel team, 125
open syllables, 110–113, 148
'or' vowel-r, 128–129
oral reading fluency, 18–19
orthographic mapping (OM), 12–13
orthography, 16
'ou' vowel team, 126–127
'ow' and 'ou' diphthongs, 127–128
oxymorons, 33–34

parents reading to students, 23–24
passage reading, 34
'ph' digraphs, 141
phonemes
   described, 14
   English as a Second Language, 22–23
   spelling, 101–103, 117
phonemic awareness
   described, 13, 14
   screening and assessment, 19
   word list, 112
phonics, 13, 14, 19, 98
phonological awareness
   described, 13, 14
   open and closed syllables, 110
phonology, 16
pocket charts, 77
power words, 36, 37
prefixes
   assimilated, 58
   bases and, 61
   described, 57–58, 59
   Latin, 59–60
progress monitoring, 17, 20, 99–100

reading aloud, 23, 34
receptive vocabulary, 27
refugees, 22
resource structure, 24–25
roots / root words, 57

Scarborough's reading rope, 11–12
schwa
   multisyllable words, 162
   vowel sound, 113–116
science of reading
   described, 11
   orthographic mapping (OM), 12–13
   Scarborough's reading rope, 11–12
   simple view of reading (SVR), 11–12
screening
   classroom intervention materials, 21–22
   described, 16
   English Language Learners (ELLs), 22–23

Index   177

intervention, 20–21
multi-tiered system of supports (MTSS), 17–18
oral reading fluency, 18–19
parents reading to students, 23–24
phonemic awareness, 19
phonics and word reading assessments, 19
purpose, 18
spelling and assessments, 19
timeline, 20
semantics, 16
silent letters
  Greek, 142
  spelling, 118–121
  worksheet, 143
simple lists, 98
simple view of reading (SVR), 11–12
soldier rule, 135–136
sound-to-symbol lists, 98
sound-to-symbol relationship, 16
speed drawing
  open and closed syllables, 111–112
  spelling, 104
  vocabulary, 37–39
spelling
  activities, 101–109
  concepts, 97, 104
  context, 97
  decoding, 94–95
  dictation, 103
  encoding, 94–95
  lesson format, 101
  lesson word lists, 98–100
  lessons, 110–142
  lessons without lists, 100–101
  marking, 100–101
  phoneme-grapheme, 101–103, 117
  pronunciation vs., 65–65
  purpose of teaching, 95–96
  teacher's relationship with, 93–94
  tests, 99–100
  worksheets, 143–146
spelling assessments, 17–18, 19, 93, 97

spelling BINGO, 107–108
stressed syllables
  activity, 75
  described, 63
  worksheet, 81
structured language and literacy
  concepts, 16
  described, 15
  hallmarks, 16
student built matrices, 76
suffixes
  bases and, 61
  derivational, 58
  described, 57–58, 59
  foundations, 65
  inflexed, 58
  Latin, 59–60
  words that end in 'e', 69–70
  words that end in 'y', 70–73
summative assessments, 17
syllabication
  steps, 149
  teaching, 150–151
syllables
  described, 16
  open and closed, 110–113, 148
  rules, 147–148
  stressed, 63, 75, 81
synonyms
  described, 32
  spelling challenge, 104
  word bank, 41
  worksheet, 54
syntax, 16

'tch' complex consonants, 135–137
teaching reading
  age level material, 10
  complex behaviours, 11
  declining reading abilities, 9
  knowledge and strategies around, 10
  readers' confidence, 10
  skill spread, 8
  teaching content and, 9–10
tier 1 words, 29, 98–99
tier 2, words, 29, 30, 98–99
tier 3, words, 29, 98–99

trigraphs
  described, 126, 135
  'igh', 126
universal screener, 17
'ur' vowel-r, 128–129
vocabulary
  activities, 34–42
  basic interpersonal communication skills (BICS), 29–30
  BINGO cards, 42
  cognitive academic language proficiency (CALP), 29–30
  described, 13, 15, 27
  expressive, 27
  functional, 31–32
  learning in context, 31
  learning progression, 27–29
  lessons, 43–46
  receptive, 27
  stretching, 34–35
  tier 1, 29, 98–99
  tier 2, 29, 30, 98–99
  tier 3, 29, 98–99
  word storage for retrieval, 30–31
  worksheets, 47
vowel-consonant-e (magic 'e'), 116–118, 148
vowel-r, 128–129, 148
vowel teams
  'ai' and 'ay', 122–123
  'aw' and 'au', 126
  chart, 159
  described, 121
  diphthongs 'oi' and 'oy', 127
  diphthongs 'ow' and 'ou', 127–128
  'ee' and 'ea', 124–125
  'oa' and 'ow', 123–124
  'oo', 125
  'ou', 126–127
  syllable rule, 148
  teaching, 121–122
  trigraph 'igh', 126
  vowel-r, 128–129
  word lists, 121, 123–129

wb (silent letter), 118–121
Wear a Word Day, 41

weird words, 80
word bank, 41, 52–54, 61, 63, 73
Word Families activity, 107
word grid, 39–40
word lists
  academic, 30
  'c' (hard and soft), 131–132
  camel, 157
  'ch' digraphs, 141
  consonant-le, 140
  described, 8
  'g' (hard and soft), 135
  Greek words, 142
  lesson, 98–100
  lion, 159
  multisyllable words with affixes, 162
  open and closed syllables, 113
  'ph' digraphs, 141
  phonemic awareness, 112
  rabbit, 153
  schwa, 116
  silent letters, 121, 142
  sound-to-symbol, 98
  'tch' and 'dge', 137
  tiger, 156
  vowel-consonant-e, 118
  vowel teams, 121, 123–129
  'y' sounds, 142
word of the day, 42
word play, 64
word reading
  activity, 112
  assessments, 19
  multisyllable words, 110–111
Word Seekers activity, 106
word sorts
  hard and soft 'c', 145–146
  morpheme, 79–80
  vocabulary, 41
word / speed drawing, 37–39, 104, 111–112
word storage for retrieval, 30–31
Wordle, 104

'y' ending words, 70–73
'y' sounds, 141–142
You're the Editor activity, 105